Twayne's English Authors Series

EDITOR OF THIS VOLUME

Sylvia E. Bowman

Indiana University

Lord Byron

Second Edition

TEAS 78

Lord Byron

LORD BYRON

By PAUL G. TRUEBLOOD
Willamette University

SECOND EDITION

TWAYNE PUBLISHERS
A DIVISION OF G. K. HALL & CO., BOSTON

Library of Congress Cataloging in Publication Data

Trueblood, Paul Graham.
    Lord Byron.

    (Twayne's English authors series ; TEAS 78)
    Bibliography: p. 185-90
    Includes index.
    1. Byron, George Gordon Noël Byron, Baron,
1788-1824.   2. Poets, English—19th century—
Biography.   I. Title.
PR4381.T7   1977   821.7   77-10564
ISBN 0-8057-6694-4

MANUFACTURED IN THE UNITED STATES OF AMERICA

To my Wife
Helen Churchill Trueblood

Contents

About the Author

Paul G. Trueblood, a Romanticism specialist and distinguished Byron scholar, holds the B.A. degree from Willamette University and the M.A. and Ph.D. degrees from Duke University. He is author of *The Flowering of Byron's Genius* (1945), a pioneering study of *Don Juan,* Byron's masterpiece, and Twayne's English Authors Series *Lord Byron* (1969). He is now editing a symposium book, *Byron in Europe: The Interplay of Poetry and Politics,* in collaboration with Byronists in ten European countries. Dr. Trueblood is a founding member and member of the board of directors of the American Byron Society. He has participated in Byron Seminars in England and Greece sponsored by the International Byron Society. In 1975 he addressed The Byron Society in the House of Lords in London on the 163rd anniversary of Byron's maiden speech in Parliament.

Dr. Trueblood has taught at the University of Idaho, University of Washington, University of Oregon, University of British Columbia, and at Willamette University where he was Professor of English and Chairman of the English Department from 1955 to 1971, becoming Professor Emeritus in 1971.

Preface

A genuine revival of interest in the life and work of Lord Byron was spurred by the publication at the turn of the twentieth century of *The Works of Lord Byron: Letters and Journals* (six volumes) and *Poetry* (seven volumes), edited by Rowland E. Prothero and Ernest Hartley Coleridge. Following the publication by Claude M. Fuess of *Lord Byron As A Satirist In Verse* (1912), a pioneering survey of Byron's satire, several significant biographical and critical studies of Byron appeared; and many of these publications were in observance of the centennial of the poet's death in 1824. Such studies as Ethel Mayne's *Byron* (1924), Samuel Chew's *Byron in England* (1924), Harold Nicolson's *Byron: The Last Journey* (1924), John Drinkwater's *The Pilgrim of Eternity* (1925), and Helene Richter's *Lord Byron: Persönlichkeit und Werk* (1929) heralded the long-needed re-interpretation of Byron.

From the 1930's onward, an increasing number of important contributions to the understanding of Byron, both as a man and as a poet, have appeared. Representative are the studies, chronologically, by Charles Du Bos, Andre Maurois, W.J. Calvert, Peter Quennell, E. F. Boyd, Paul G. Trueblood, W.A. Borst, Iris Origo, W.W. Pratt, Ernest J. Lovell Jr., C.L. Cline, G.W. Knight, Robert Escarpit, G.M. Ridenour, Paul West, D.L. Moore, Peter Thorslev, W.H. Marshall, Andrew Rutherford, E.E. Bostetter, M.K. Joseph, L.A. Marchand, Robert F. Gleckner, W. Paul Elledge, Jerome J. McGann, M.G. Cooke, John D. Jump, Bernard Blackstone, and Charles E. Robinson. Eight of these works are full-length, general critical studies of Byron by Calvert, Escarpit, Rutherford, Marshall, Joseph, Marchand, McGann, and Cooke.

Two of the greatest contributions to modern Byron scholarship appeared in 1957. Professor Leslie A. Marchand placed all present and future Byron scholars in debt to his magisterial, indispensable biography of Byron. In this magnificent three-volume work, we have Byron speaking for himself. The other major contribution was the monumental *Variorum Don Juan,* edited by Truman Guy

Steffan and Willis W. Pratt; for their four volumes include an exhaustive treatment of composition and structure, the definitive text with *variae lectiones,* and a comprehensive survey of critical commentary on *Don Juan.*

The *raison d'etre* of this revised edition of the Twayne Series *Byron* is the appearance in the late 1960's and in the early 1970's of a cluster of superb critical studies of Byron by Professors Gleckner, Elledge, McGann, and Cooke, and a definitive one-volume biography of the poet by Professor Marchand. Furthermore, what is certain to be the major contribution to Byron scholarship in the twentieth century is now appearing: *Byron's Letters and Journals,* edited by Professor Marchand, and *Byron's Complete Poetical Works,* edited by Professor McGann. These definitive multivolume works will supersede the turn-of-the-century Coleridge-Prothero edition.

Another evidence of the resurgence of interest in Byron has been the recent revival of The Byron Society, originally founded as "The Byron Club" in London on January 22, 1876, at the Temple Club, 37 Arundel Street, which premises, known in Byron's day as the Crown and Anchor, served as the meeting place for the Greek Committee that invited Byron in 1823 to be its representative in Greece. The Society received further impetus in 1888, the centennial year of the poet's birth, at the instigation of King George I of Greece who desired to preserve the memory of the great Romantic poet who died in the Greek War of Independence.

The Byron Society flourished during the early decades of the twentieth century, numbering Sir Winston Churchill among its members, until it ceased its activities at the outbreak of World War II. The Byron Society was re-founded in 1971 by the late Dennis Walwin Jones, and it has since grown into The International Byron Society headquartered in London with branches in twenty-three countries. The Society, which has as its objectives the promotion of interest and research in the life and work of Byron, publishes a journal devoted to Byron biographical, critical, and editorial scholarship; holds annual international seminars; and arranges tours to countries with which the poet was associated.

On December 20, 1976, the *London Times* announced the discovery by Barclays Bank of a trunk that belonged to Scrope Davies, a crony of Byron, who had stored in this receptacle manuscripts of Byron and Shelley. On December 21, *The New York Times* hailed the discovery as "the literary find of the century," for the discovered material included the original manuscript of Byron's *Childe Harold,* Canto III, and fourteen unknown letters of Byron. These discoveries were a spur to the widespread, increasing interest in Byron throughout the world.

Of all the English authors of major rank, Byron has been perhaps the most misunderstood by the general public. The purpose of this modest book is to encourage understanding and appreciation of the personality and work of one of the most attractive and "modern" of the Romantic poets. I would like to prompt the student and general reader to go to Marchand for Byron's life, to the several attractive modern editions of the poet's work for enjoyment of his poetry, and to the many excellent critical studies for more extensive appraisal of Byron's rightful place in English and European literature.

Byron's life and work are inseparable in even greater degree than with most authors. Bernard Blackstone in *The Lost Travelers* (1962) asserts that Byron's life and poetry exhibit "a completely integrated relationship. The one constantly expresses or anticipates the other." Jerome McGann in *Fiery Dust* (1968) writes, "Indeed, it seems to be a law in Byron's poetry that anything goes so long as it serves to advance our sense of Byron's immediate personal presence." And Edward E. Bostetter in his introduction to the Rinehart Byron declares that there is a "vital relationship" between Byron's poetry and his life that is "unequalled in literature." Convinced that an understanding of Byron, "The Man," is prerequisite to a critical assessment of Byron, "The Poet," I have given considerable attention to Byron's life. Herein I am profoundly indebted to Marchand's definitive biography which inevitably reduces any subsequent biographical effort to an inadequate paraphrase.

In my consideration of Byron's chief poetical works, I have dealt with the genesis of each work, its subject matter, structure, style, and relationship to the poet's total poetic production. Likewise, I have endeavored to present some of the most pertinent and perceptive critical views of Byron now current among scholars. I have concluded the book with a brief summary of Byron's contribution to literature and to society. My scholarly debts, which are legion, are adequately acknowledged, I trust, in the notes and bibliography. I am especially grateful to the University of Chicago Press for permission to quote extensively from Professor McGann's

Fiery Dust (1968) and *Don Juan in Context* (1976) which I regard as two of the most important books about Byron to appear in the twentieth century.

It was my privilege, preparatory to writing and then revising this book, to follow Byron's trail through Britain, Portugal, Spain, Belgium, the Rhineland, Switzerland, Italy, and Greece during my two-year residence in Europe. One can readily agree with Professor Marchand that the traveler following Byron's footsteps is struck by the extent and persistence of the poet's European reputation. And nowhere is this view more evident than in Greece where Byron has been a revered national hero ever since his death in 1824 in the Greek War of Independence. Evidence of the widespread political influence of Byron throughout the Continent is a symposium volume now in preparation, *Byron in Europe: The Interplay of Poetry and Politics,* which I am editing in collaboration with Byronists in ten European countries.

Byron materials and memorabilia which I have been privileged to examine during my travels include those of the Nottingham Public Library; the Roe-Byron Collection at Newstead Abbey; the Wren Library, Cambridge University; the Bodleian Library, Oxford University; the British Museum Reading and Manuscript Rooms; the Murray Byron Collection, 50 Albemarle Street, London; the Gamba Papers in the Biblioteca Classense in Ravenna; the Keats-Shelley Memorial Library in Rome; the Gennadius Library in Athens; and the City Museum at Missolonghi, where Byron died.

Among the European Byronists to whom I am grateful for friendly interest and encouragement are the late Professor V. de Sola Pinto of the University of Nottingham; Miss Lucy I. Edwards of the Nottingham Public Library; the late Sir John Murray and Mr. John Grey Murray of London; Professor Andrew Rutherford of the University of Aberdeen; Mrs. Doris Langley Moore of London; the late Dennis Walwin Jones, and Mrs. Elma Dangerfield, Mr. Ian Scott-Kilvert, and Mr. Michael Rees, all of The Byron Society, London; the Marchesa Iris Origo of Rome; Signora Vera Cacciatore, curator of the Keats House in Rome; and Dr. George Kournoutos of the Greek Ministry of Culture, Athens. Special thanks are due to Dr. Francis R. Walton, Director of the Gennadius Library, Athens, and to his assistant, Miss Beatrice Demetracopoulo, for every courtesy, and to Professor C.W.J. Eliot, of the American School of Classical Studies, Athens, for sharing his knowledge of Athens in the time of Lord Byron.

Here may I express appreciation to the Contessa Cini di Pianzano and her daughters for their delightful hospitality at Filetto near Ravenna. The Contessa, whose husband is a descendant of the Gamba Family, showed us mementoes of Teresa Guiccioli and told us of the destruction by the Nazis of the beautiful Villa Gamba where Lord Byron was a frequent guest. In Greece, where my wife and I twice resided for eight months, the hospitality and friendly aid of the Greeks knew no bounds.

I want to express my appreciation to the Administration and Board of Trustees of Willamette University for the sabbatical leave which enabled me to initiate this project and to the Atkinson Committee for the generous travel grant which made it possible for me to pursue the project in Europe. Finally, I want to thank my wife, Helen, who has shared fully in all the labors and delights of following the fascinating trail of Lord Byron throughout Great Britain and the Continent.

PAUL G. TRUEBLOOD

Willamette University

Chronology

1788   George Gordon Byron born, January 22, in London, son of Captain John ("Mad Jack") Byron and Mrs. Byron (formerly Catherine Gordon of Gight).

1790   Mrs. Byron, her fortune spent by her wastrel husband, takes her son to Aberdeen.

1791   Captain Byron, father of George Gordon, dies at thirty-six in France.

1792   George Gordon attends day school in Aberdeen.

1794   Becomes heir presumptive to title of grand-uncle, Fifth Lord Byron ("Wicked Lord").

1798   Inherits title on death of grand-uncle; an English peer, Byron, aged ten, moves to Newstead Abbey, Nottinghamshire, Byron family seat.

1798-   Tutored in Nottingham by Rogers; club-foot treated by
1799   quack doctor, Lavender; mistreated by Scotch maid.

1799-   Attends boarding school at Dulwich, near London.
1801

1801-   Byron attends Harrow School; spends vacations with Mrs.
1805   Byron at Southwell.

1803   First love, Mary Chaworth of Annesley Hall, grand-niece of Lord Chaworth who had been killed by the "Wicked" Lord Byron in a duel.

1804   Begins correspondence with his half-sister, Augusta.

1805   Enters Trinity College, Cambridge.

1806   *Fugitive Pieces,* first poems, privately printed.

1807   *Hours of Idleness;* drawn into Cambridge circle of young intellectuals and political liberals.

1808   *Hours of Idleness* attacked in *Edinburgh Review.* Byron receives master's degree at Cambridge in July.

1809   Takes seat, March 13, in House of Lords. Publishes retaliatory satire, *English Bards and Scotch Reviewers.* With Hobhouse departs in July for journey through Portugal, Spain,

Albania, and Greece. Completes first canto of *Childe Harold* in Athens.

1810 Finishes second canto of *Childe Harold,* March 28. Travels in Turkey and Greece. Swims Hellespont, May 3. Lives in Athens.

1811 Returns to England in July. Mother dies in August.

1812 Gives three liberal speeches in House of Lords. *Childe Harold,* published by John Murray in March, brings immediate fame. Affair with Lady Caroline Lamb.

1813 Begins affair in June with half-sister, Augusta Leigh. Publishes first Oriental tales, *Giaour* and *Bride of Abydos.*

1814 Publishes *Corsair* and *Lara.* Becomes engaged in September to Anabella Milbanke.

1815 Byron marries Annabella Milbanke, January 2. Daughter, Augusta Ada, born December 10.

1816 Lady Byron leaves Byron January 15; formal separation signed April 21. Byron, on April 25, leaves England forever. Journeys up Rhine; spends summer in Switzerland in company of Shelley, Mary Godwin, and Claire Clairmont. With Hobhouse tours Alps and travels to Italy. Publishes Canto III of *Childe Harold* and *Prisoner of Chillon.* Begins *Manfred.*

1817 Allegra, daughter by Claire Clairmont, born January 12. Residing in Venice, Byron continues liaison with Marianna Segati. Visits Florence and Rome; completes *Manfred* and works on fourth canto of *Childe Harold;* experiments in *Beppo* with colloquial *ottava rima* on theme of Venetian life.

1818 Begins liaison with Margarita Cogni; abandons himself to dissipation without losing literary energy. *Beppo* published in February. *Childe Harold* IV published in April. Begins *Don Juan;* finishes Canto I in September.

1819 Weary of debauchery, Byron meets Teresa, Countess Guiccioli, in April. Strong mutual attraction leads to last liaison. Spends fall with Teresa at La Mira and continues *Don Juan.* Thomas Moore visits Byron and is given gift of Byron's memoirs. *Don Juan* I and II published in July.

1820 Byron lives in Guiccioli palace in Ravenna. Continues *Don Juan;* writes first of poetic dramas, *Marino Faliero.* Teresa's application for separation from Count Guiccioli granted by

Pope in July. Byron visits Teresa at Gamba family villa at Filetto; becomes involved in revolutionary Carbonari struggle against Austrian rule in Italy.

1821 Carbonari movement defeated. Gambas, Teresa's family, banished to Pisa. Outbreak of Greek war for independence interests Byron. *Don Juan* III, IV, V, published in August; promises Teresa not to continue *Don Juan*. In September writes *Vision of Judgment*. Joins Gambas and Shelley in Pisa in November. *Cain* published in December.

1822 British outcry against *Cain* and *Don Juan* increases. Teresa consenting, Byron resumes *Don Juan*. Leigh Hunt and family lodged in Byron's Pisa house. Shelley drowns in Bay of Lerici. Byron joins exiled Gambas in Genoa. Byron's thoughts turn toward Greece. *Vision of Judgment* published in October. British outcry excessive. Byron changes to John Hunt as publisher.

1823 London Greek Committee enlists Byron's aid on behalf of Greece. Byron sails in July for Greece with Teresa's brother, Pietro Gamba; welcomed in Cephalonia. Byron severely ill after strenuous excursion to Ithaca. Sets sail for Missolonghi on December 30. *Don Juan,* VI to XIV, published.

1824 Byron hailed in Missolonghi on January 4 as a deliverer. On January 22 writes "On This Day I Complete My Thirty-Sixth Year." Tries to form artillery corps to send against Turkish-held stronghold of Lepanto. Despite constant reverses and deteriorating health, Byron pours his fortune and energy into uncertain Greek cause. Cantos XV and XVI of *Don Juan* published in March. Byron gravely ill on April 9; incompetent doctors insist on repeated bleedings; dies on April 19. Mourned by the Greeks as national hero; regarded throughout Europe as "the Trumpet Voice of Liberty," Lord Byron is buried July 16 in Hucknall Torkard Church near Newstead.

CHAPTER 1

1788–1805 Childhood and Schooldays

GEORGE Gordon Byron was born with a caul and clubfoot on January 22, 1788, in London, the son of Captain John ("Mad Jack") Byron and Mrs. Byron, formerly Catherine Gordon of Gight. Mrs. Byron, her fortune spent by her wastrel husband, had returned in December from France for her accouchement. The spendthrift Captain Byron followed a few weeks later but, engaged in cautiously dodging creditors, was not present at his son's birth.

This marriage was the handsome, dissolute, fortune-hunting Captain Byron's second. In 1778 he had eloped with the beautiful Lady Carmarthen, wife of Francis, Marquis of Leeds; and he had married her the next year following the divorce which the Marquis had secured by an act of Parliament. Taking his heiress to France to escape from scandal and creditors, Captain Byron riotously squandered Lady Carmarthen's fortune until her death in 1784, leaving him with an infant daughter, Augusta, born in 1783, the poet's half-sister. The carefree Captain then returned to England in search of another heiress. In 1785 he met and married Catherine Gordon of Gight, a plain-faced, naïve, but proud, Scottish country girl with a fortune in excess of twenty-three thousand pounds. In three harried, dissolute years, moving from place to place to escape creditors and bailiffs, Captain Byron so exhausted his wife's fortune that she was virtually destitute at the time of her son's birth in London in 1788.

This madcap behavior of Captain John Byron was quite in keeping with the history of his ancestors. The Byrons traced their ancestry to the Buruns in the time of William the Conqueror. In the sixteenth century Henry VIII awarded to Sir John Byron the picturesque Newstead Abbey in Nottinghamshire and extensive holdings in the surrounding countryside and Sherwood Forest. A later Sir

John Byron was created Baron Byron of Rochdale by Charles I. After the Civil War the Byrons regained their ancestral estate of Newstead Abbey. William, the fifth Lord Byron, was notorious for his extravagances and rakish behavior. These included the attempted abduction of an actress, the building of a miniature Gothic castle and two turreted forts on the banks of the lake at Newstead, the staging of mock naval battles on the lake, and the despoiling of the magnificent oak forest around the Abbey. In his mid-forties he killed in a duel his cousin and neighbor, William Chaworth of Annesley Hall. Thenceforth, and until the end of his life as a virtual recluse, the fifth Lord Byron was known as the "Wicked Lord."

His brother, John, grandfather of the poet, went to sea at seventeen, endured harrowing adventures of shipwreck and hardship which he recounted in his *Narrative* (1768), married his first cousin, supported a mistress in London, and rose to the rank of rear-admiral, coming to be known as "Foul-weather Jack" because of the storms he invariably encountered. Before his death in 1786 he disinherited his eldest son, Captain John ("Mad Jack") Byron, father of the poet, whose notorious prodigalities exceeded those of his sire.

The hapless Catherine Gordon, mother of the poet, came from a line of Scottish Gordons whose irregular conduct easily matched, if not exceeded, that of the Byrons. She was descended from Sir William Gordon of Gight, north of Aberdeen, whose mother was Princess Anabella Stuart, daughter of James I of Scotland. Throughout the sixteenth century the Gordons were distinguished among the Scottish lairds for the lawlessness and violence of their behavior. During the eighteenth century, as the hotbloodedness of the clans abated, the conduct of the Gordons became more moderate and civilized. George Gordon, the twelfth laird of Gight, had three daughters of whom only Catherine Gordon survived his death in 1779 to become heir to the Gordon fortune.[1]

I *Aberdeen*

Ten years later, as the wife of Captain Byron, finding herself destitute with a lame baby to care for and deserted by her worthless husband, Mrs. Byron took her little boy to her native Aberdeen. Here she managed an uncertain and cramped existence, her husband returning from time to time to wheedle a loan from his exasperated but always indulgent wife, until in 1791, in France, Captain Byron died, aged thirty-six. Grief-stricken over the loss of her faithless "Johnny Byron," Mrs. Byron devoted herself unstintingly to the care of her young, lame son. Only her poverty prevented her taking the little boy to London to consult a medical expert with regard to a proper shoe for the deformed right foot. Little George, very sensitive to his lameness, flew into a temper if anyone openly called it to attention; but otherwise he ignored it in his preoccupation with childish play. Mrs. Byron aggravated his sensitiveness by upbraiding him angrily for his deformity and by showering him with kisses in moods of excessive indulgence.

Inevitably, the boy very early was affected by his mother's extremely vacillating moods, vehement temper, fierce pride, and strong prejudices and predilections. How much the child was influenced by his nurse, Agnes Gray, "a pious, Bible-reading Presbyterian,"[2] is a matter of speculation. However, it seems probable that the kind, well-meaning woman had much to do with instilling into the boy's impressionable mind the strict Calvinistic creed which never deserted the poet, and with initiating his genuine admiration of the Bible and his thorough familiarity with it.

In the summer of 1794 an event occurred which profoundly affected the entire life of the young George Gordon Byron. William Byron, the grandson of the "Wicked Lord" Byron, died, leaving the six-and-one-half-year-old George heir presumptive to the title and estates of his grand-uncle, the fifth Lord Byron. Mrs. Byron now placed her son in the Aberdeen Grammar School. Although not at first distinguished in his studies, he early manifested a strong bent for reading. The *Arabian Nights,* Cervantes, Smollett's novels, and especially histories and travels were among his favorites.

He later wrote his publisher, John Murray, that he had read the books of the Old Testament "through and through before I was eight years old."[3] He was particularly fascinated by the dramatic stories of the Bible, such as that of Cain and Abel, a fact he was later to acknowledge in his own drama of *Cain.* Marchand suggests that the poet's lifelong obsession with the idea that he was predestined to innate and inescapable evil was shaped by the Old Testament conception, nurtured by the Calvinistic teaching of his nurse and his Presbyterian tutors, and strengthened by his increasing awareness of the dark history of his own ancestors.[4]

Outwardly, according to Thomas Moore, his first biographer, young George's manner was that of a normal boy, "lively, warmhearted, and high-spirited . . . passionate and resentful, but affectionate and . . . fearless . . . 'always more ready to give a blow than to take one.'"[5] He early manifested the extraordinary capacity for friendship and strong devotion to the underdog which characterized him throughout life. Always ready to thrash any boy who ridiculed his lameness, he was just as prompt to defend any younger boy from the persecution of his fellows. He entered freely, despite his handicap, into all boyish games and sports, including swimming in the estuaries of the Dee and Don, and even the North Sea itself. Here began Byron's initiation into his favorite sport which was one day to be climaxed with his swimming of the Hellespont. Likewise, in his eighth year, the youngster was privileged to visit and ramble about in the Scottish highlands north of Aberdeen where his deep and lasting affection for "Lachin y Gair" and other beautiful mountains of Scotland was formed.

About this time, young George, precocious in his passions as he was otherwise, experienced his first love affair. He met and felt all the pangs of boyish love for his distant cousin, the pretty, dark-haired Mary Duff. Later, when he was sixteen, he was nearly convulsed by the news that Mary Duff was married.

II *Young Lord Byron*

In 1798, upon the death of his grand-uncle, the "Wicked Lord" Byron, George Gordon Byron became the sixth Baron Byron of Rochdale, inheriting the Nottingham estates of the Byrons. Proud of his ancestry on both sides, as his mother had taught him to be, the lad, an English peer at the age of ten, was deeply moved when his new title, "Dominus de Byron," was first employed by the master in the Grammar School. "Unable to give utterance to the usual answer 'adsum,'" Moore tells us, "he stood silent amid the general stare of his schoolfellows, and, at last, burst into tears."[6]

Late in the summer of 1798, Mrs. Byron and the young lord, accompanied by May Gray (who had replaced her sister, Agnes, now married), left Aberdeen and journeyed by coach to Nottinghamshire in England. Both mother and son were delighted with the

Byrons' ancestral estate of Newstead — with its romantic Gothic Abbey, sweeping grounds, great oaks, and lakes — despite the sad state of disrepair in which the old lord had left it; and they were determined to live there. John Hanson, the London solicitor who was to remain Byron's practical guardian and general business agent, reluctantly agreed that Mrs. Byron and her son could live at Newstead until desperately needed repairs could be made and an appropriate renter found for the manor.

The young lord — happy in his role as a landed nobleman, and proud of the Byron arms with the mermaid and chestnut horses surmounting the motto, "Crede Byron" — took boyish pleasure in the play fort and Gothic castle on the lake, in the palatial proportions of the rooms of the manor, and in the spaciousness of the surrounding fields and forest. To celebrate his new status, and to symbolize the hoped-for flourishing of his noble career, the young lord planted an oak tree on the green that sloped to the lower lake.

By 1799 young Byron was living in Nottingham with the Parkyns family and was being tutored in Latin, French, and mathematics by a young American, Dummer Rogers. At the same time he was receiving very painful treatments for his lame foot by a quack doctor, Lavender, who attempted to straighten the clubfoot by rubbing it with oil and by screwing it up in a wooden device. At this time the young lord was also subjected to the improper advances of the maid May Gray, who had been left in Nottingham to look after the lad while he was being "tortured" by Lavender. We learn from Leslie Marchand the unsavoury details of the mistreatment of the boy by May Gray which included drunkenness, neglect, beatings, and sexual liberties. When Byron revealed this situation to his guardian, Hanson immediately advised Mrs. Byron; and May Gray was dismissed — but not before the boy had suffered psychological injury in the premature initiation into sex-play and the development of his precocious sexual propensities.[7] Looking back on his youth, Byron wrote in his "Detached Thoughts" (1821): "My passions were developed very early — so early, that few would believe me, if I were to state the period, and the facts which accompanied it."[8]

In the summer of 1799 Hanson took young Byron to London to obtain expert medical advice about proper treatment of the lame foot and to arrange for the systematic education of the young peer. The diagnosis of Dr. Matthew Baillie, an eminent anatomist, of the boy's deformity corresponds exactly with that of the most reliable witnesses, including Mrs. Byron, who had said, "George's foot turns inward, and it is the right foot; he walks quite on the side of his foot." Byron's lameness, Marchand authoritatively concludes, has been accurately described by Dr. James Kemble, who made a thorough examination of all the evidence including Byron's boots at John Murray's in London, as a "congenital clubfoot of the Talipes Equino-varus type, affecting the right foot only."[9] On the advice of Dr. Baillie, a special boot was constructed by Mr. Sheldrake of the Strand. To the corrective boot, a brace later was added; it was devised by Dr. Maurice Laurie of Bartholomew's Close, who thenceforth continued the practical care of the case. Byron was impatient with this device and often neglected to wear it or discarded it when it impeded his activity.

By September the young lord was comfortably settled in Dr. Glennie's small boarding school, selected for him by Hanson, at Dulwich near London. Although Byron was less well prepared than the other boys in Latin grammar, Dr. Glennie, a Scotsman found him well advanced in history and poetry and in his intimate knowledge of the Old Testament. Apparently Dr. Glennie was as charmed by the youth as was Hanson, who declared that Byron possessed ability, quickness of conception, and discrimination far beyond his years — as well as a maturity which dictated that "choice indeed must be the Company that is selected for him."[10]

Mrs. Byron came to London at the beginning of 1800, ostensibly on business but chiefly to be near her son. With Hanson she called on Byron's kinsman, the Earl of Carlisle, who had reluctantly consented to be the titular guardian of the young Lord Byron but only in an advisory capacity. Mrs. Byron's impulsive behavior, capricious temper, and willingness to interfere with her son's education throughout her stay in London were an annoyance to both of the boy's guardians, a harassment to Dr. Glennie, and a constant embarrassment to the boy himself.

During the summer vacation of 1800, while living with his mother at Nottingham and Newstead, Byron experienced his second boyish infatuation with his first cousin Margaret Parker, "...one of the most beautiful of evanescent beings," he wrote later, who inspired his "first dash into poetry." "I have long forgotten the verses, but it would be difficult for me to forget her. Her dark eyes! her long eye-lashes! ... I was then about twelve.... She looked as if she had been made out of a rainbow — all beauty and peace."[11]

In this experience, essentially like the earlier Mary Duff affair, and in the very different one with May Gray, Marchand sees the very crux of "two parallel developments in Byron's relations with women, both awakening his sensibilities at an abnormally precocious age, and both with tremendous implications to his later life." The Duff and Parker affairs stimulated his "dash into poetry," and ever thereafter symbolized for him the "ideally beautiful unpossessed love" that he sought throughout his life. The May Gray experience — the premature stimulation of sexual awareness — nurtured in him the disillusionment, melancholy, and disgust which follow when the actual experience fails to achieve the ideal. Marchand concludes: "The first carried him into love with young girls and boys; the second into the cynical search for 'fine animals' like the baker's wife in Venice."[12]

III *Byron at Harrow*

Hanson, who held the young lord in high esteem, was convinced that the boy should have the advantage of the great public schools; and he readily persuaded Lord Carlisle of the same. Accordingly, Dr. Glennie was instructed to prepare Byron for Harrow. Late in April, 1801, Byron accompanied Hanson to Harrow, where he was introduced to Dr. Joseph Drury, the headmaster. Dr. Drury was impressed by the dignified, if haughty, bearing of the handsome young lord with the Classic features, auburn curls, and clear, blue-gray eyes; and he readily discerned behind the façade of shyness and reserve a genuine responsiveness to friendly and tactful treatment. He rightly concluded that the "wild mountain colt ... might be led by a silken string . . . ."[13]

Realizing that the sensitive and undisciplined youth, only recently turned thirteen, would be at a disadvantage because of his deformity and the inadequacy of his schooling, Dr. Drury placed him under the tutorship of his son, Henry Drury, one of the younger masters, and assigned him quarters in Henry Drury's house. Manly, fiercely independent, sensitive and passionate, yet with an extraordinary capacity for friendship, extreme generosity, and an almost feminine tenderness in his affections, young Byron was now thrust into the strenuous and often cruel give-and-take of one of the most famous public schools of England.

Harrow, founded in 1571 by John Lyon, was, like Eton, popular with the aristocracy. Byron's associates in 1801 included the scions of many noble families as well as a generous representation of the middle class. During his first months at Harrow, Byron hated the school in which he had to fist-fight his way into the respect and admiration of his fellow schoolmates. Wearing a shoe with a brace around the ankle, he was very sensitive about his lameness and valiantly defended himself against the ruthless taunts of the schoolboys. He soon became known as the indefatigable champion of smaller boys, some of whom remained his friends through life. He never permitted his handicap to bar him from joining in all the boyish sports, even engaging in cricket, and quite excelling the other boys in swimming. His lameness was improving under Dr. Laurie's ministrations, but the doctor was quite concerned over Byron's careless neglect of his foot.

How early Byron began to write verse is not known (except for his verse at twelve), but certainly by his fourteenth and fifteenth years he was scribbling epigrams and satiric rhymes for the amusement of his classmates and, unknown to them, engaging occasionally in more serious poetic efforts. His favorite spot at Harrow for solitary reflection and poetic composition was the "Peachey Stone," a flat, low tombstone in a corner of the Harrow churchyard of one John Peachey. On the brow of the hill overlooking the pastoral valleys and wooded hills beyond, the youthful poet composed the elegy to his beautiful cousin, Margaret Parker, "On the Death of a Young Lady." It may be that even this early he was beginning to be dimly aware of the value of poetic expression as a catharsis of the deeper emotions.

By the time he was fifteen Byron was beginning to enjoy Harrow. The headmaster, Dr. Drury, he held in high esteem, and not without reciprocation. To Lord Carlisle, Drury reported: "He has talents, my lord, which will *add lustre to his rank*."[14] The young lord was also gaining popularity among the Harrovians for his prowess as a formidable champion of younger boys, as a gay leader in all school mischief, and as an affectionate and devoted friend. At Harrow began those passionate attachments, especially to younger boys, which characterized him throughout life. Harrow favorites included Lord Clare; Earl of Delawarr; Duke of Dorset; John Wingfield; and Edward Long.

"How early Byron was aware of the sexual implications of these passionate friendships it is difficult to know," writes Marchand. But, he continues, "there is no evidence that he felt guilt or shame about any of the friendships formed at Harrow." Byron, he concludes, had strong bisexual tendencies throughout life, though, on the whole, his emotional needs were satisfied more extensively and over longer periods of his life by his relationships with women.[15] Many of his best friends witnessed to the admixture in Byron of pronounced feminine qualities of tenderness, passion, and caprice, together with all the most attractive manly attributes of courage, strength, and frankness.

Newstead being let to young Lord Grey de Ruthyn, Byron spent his summer vacations with his mother at Southwell near Nottingham. Finding village life boring, Byron rode frequently to Newstead, twelve miles away. He soon discovered a much greater attraction at Annesley Hall, nearby Newstead, in his distant cousin, Mary Chaworth, a beautiful girl of eighteen. The fifteen-year-old youth was soon passionately in love with the amiable and charming Mary, who was, no doubt, entertained by the adolescent devotion of the handsome, if awkward, youth, even though she was engaged to John Musters, a sophisticated young country squire of the neighborhood. Byron refused, in spite of Mrs. Byron's entreaties, to return to Harrow, insisting on remaining near the object of his adoration. Later he was to tell Medwin that Mary Chaworth was the "*beau idéal* of all that my youthful fancy could paint of [the] beautiful," and that she inspired all his later "fables about the celestial nature of women."[16] But, when his passion was not reciprocated, the lovelorn youth was disconsolate.

About this time Byron was subjected to an unpleasant experience which may have had far-reaching psychological effects. Lord Grey, the pampered and sensuous youthful tenant of Newstead, Byron's senior by eight years, with whom Byron was at first on amicable terms, seems to have made some sort of sexual overture to the younger lord which so shocked him that he left Newstead with the resolve never to see Lord Grey again. Though Lord Byron never disclosed the character of the offense, his later references to Grey leave no doubt about its nature.[17]

By January, 1804, Byron was, resignedly, back at Harrow, renewing his warm friendships, resuming his leadership in school mischief, and winning the gratifying praise of Dr. Drury for his pronounced oratorical ability on Speech Day. At this time Byron also began an intimate and continuing correspondence with his half-sister, Augusta, five years his senior, making her his confidante. His affection for Augusta grew as his disaffection with his mother increased; her latest folly was an infatuation with Lord Grey. Byron asked Augusta to consider him "not only as *a Brother* but as your warmest and most affectionate *Friend.* . . .you are *the nearest relation* I have in *the world both by the ties of Blood and affection.*"[18] The ever-widening gulf between Byron and his mother, who in her worst fits of temper was capable of calling him a "lame brat," impelled him ever nearer in his great need for acceptance and affection to his half-sister, Augusta.

By the spring of 1805, Byron, now seventeen and a leader in his school, was most loath to leave Harrow. He led the rebellion against George Butler, the new headmaster, chiefly out of veneration for the retiring Dr. Drury; and he achieved his ambition of playing cricket in the final game of the year against Eton. His foot was by this time so improved that he wore an ordinary boot which enclosed an inside corrective shoe for support. Harrow days, with all their passionate friendships, rowdy escapades, and oratorical achievements, were now over. But Byron was not enthusiastic about the prospect of Cambridge; he preferred Oxford.

When his mother, whom he described to Augusta as a " *happy* compound of derangement and Folly," taunted him in August, 1805, with the news that his beloved Mary Chaworth was married, Byron was pale and silent. But he expressed his deep emotion in verse:

> Hills of Annesley, Bleak and Barren,
>   Where my thoughtless Childhood stray'd,
> How the northern Tempests, warring,   5 1-2
>   Howl about thy tufted Shade!
>
> Now no more, the Hours beguiling,
>   Former favourite Haunts I see;
> Now no more my Mary smiling,
>   Makes ye seem a Heaven to me.

CHAPTER 2

1805–1809 Cambridge, Hours of Idleness *and* English Bards

W HEN Lord Byron entered Trinity College of Cambridge University in 1805 at the age of seventeen and a half, he halfheartedly tried to assume the dissipated role expected of young aristocrats of his day; but he admitted later that he "could not share in the common-place libertinism of the place and time without disgust."[1] His closest friends at Cambridge were not nobles but commoners such as his Harrow friend Edward Long and William Bankes. With them he rode, swam at Grantchester, wined and dined, and shared the enjoyment of reading.

Early in 1806 Byron wrote to his confidante, Augusta, of his prevailing mood of melancholy, the secret cause of which he only hinted. Deprived of the idealized loves of his youth (Mary Duff, Margaret Parker, and Mary Chaworth), and by nature preferring to concentrate his affections rather than spread them widely, Byron at this time formed romantic attachments to Edward Long and to John Edleston, a choir boy of Trinity Chapel, two years his junior. There is little reason to doubt, thinks Marchand, that Byron's feeling at this time for younger men and boys, whatever it may have been later following his Eastern travels, was, in Byron's own words, "a violent, though *pure,* love and passion," — a genuine romantic attachment. His lines "To E———," written at Cambridge, were probably addressed to Edleston.[2]

About this time, the eighteen-year-old Byron, who began taking fencing lessons in London with Henry Angelo and boxing lessons with Gentleman Jackson, the noted pugilist, entered an entirely new milieu. In this sporting and theatrical world he was soon ini-

29

tiated into all the usual dissipations, including relationships with sophisticated *demimondes.* Preferring London life, swimming at Worthing on the Sussex coast, or engaging in amateur theatricals at Southwell, Byron skipped the fall term at Cambridge. Much of his attention was given to preparing a small volume of his poems which he had written at Harrow and afterward. The volume, entitled *Fugitive Pieces,* was privately printed without Byron's name by John Ridge of Newark in November, 1806.

The surprising fact about these early poems is that among the romantic and melancholy verses, which met with the approval of his more serious friends, were an almost equal number of realistic and satiric poems, as well as a few frankly erotic ones. "To a Lady Who Presented the Author a Lock of Hair, Braided with his Own, and Appointed a Night in December to Meet Him in the Garden" significantly foreshadows Byron's later sophisticated serio-comic mode. Of the amorous poems, "To Mary" most distressed Byron's friend and mentor, the Reverent John T. Becher, a Nottingham-shire vicar who had encouraged his poetic efforts.

Although Byron defended his poems as "the simple Truth," much as he later defended *Don Juan,* he deferred to his friend's advice, withdrew and destroyed the copies he had distributed, and at once began preparing a more "chaste" edition of his poems. He omitted some of the more erotic poems and passages; added the lyric, "The First Kiss of Love," and his nostalgic reminiscences of Harrow, "Childish Recollections"; and produced, in his words, a "*vastly* correct and miraculously chaste" volume of juvenilia, *Poems on Various Occasions,* of which one hundred copies were printed by Ridge in January, 1807. Prolonging his absence from Cambridge into the spring, Byron distributed copies of his poems among friends and continued writing new ones.

Byron's tendency to corpulency, inherited from his mother, was so intolerable to him that he began at this time a severe reducing regimen. Only five feet, eight and one-half inches in height, he had reached the excessive weight of over two hundred pounds in the fall of 1806. By strenuous exercise, rigorous dieting, and the use of physic, he had reduced his weight by 1808 to one hundred and fifty-five pounds and by 1811 to less than one hundred and forty. This attractive slenderness Byron maintained, by the continued practice of his harsh regimen, until his period of relaxed dissipation in Venice in 1818.[3]

Byron's stay in Southwell was occupied with flirting with the local belles and poetizing; his manner was characteristically gay and animated, with little if any manifestation of the sentimental and melancholy mood which soon came to be associated with the youthful poet. He stayed on in Southwell to complete his first volume of poetry intended for the general public.

I Hours of Idleness

Lord Byron's first venture into public authorship, *Hours of Idleness,* appeared in June, 1807. Undistinguished save for technical facility and largely imitative of eighteenth-century Romantic or neo-Classical elements, these early verses of his Harrow, Southwell, and Cambridge days, reveal, as Andrew Rutherford points out, Byron's youthful taste in poetry, his persisting tendency to romanticize his personal experiences and emotions, and an interesting range of feelings and attitudes.[4] In this polyglot collection, the youthful poet's tastes and obvious influences include, from the preceding century, Thomas Gray, William Cowper, Thomas Chatterton, James Macpherson's *Ossian,* Robert Burns, and other "early Romantics," and from his own era, Thomas Moore and Walter Scott. Byron's chief admiration from the Augustan period was Alexander Pope, whom he revered throughout life.

"On the Death of a Young Lady," addressed to his cousin Margaret Parker, is representative of the elegiac mood of many of the poems. The first of the six stanzas reads:

> Hush'd are the winds, and still the evening gloom,
>   Not e'en a zephyr wanders through the grove,
> Whilst I return to view my Margaret's tomb,   4
>   And scatter flowers on the dust I love.

This poem is early evidence not only of his inclination to romanticize his experiences but also of his dawning awareness of the value of poetry as a catharsis of the deeper emotions. An example of the second use of poetry is the lines, "Hills of Annesely."

Other examples of the rather wide variety of feelings and attitudes displayed by these verses are the opening piece, "On Leaving Newstead," lamenting that "Thou, the hall of my Fathers, art gone to decay"; a number of school exercises and translations; nostalgic poems such as "Lachin Y Gair," recalling his happy boyhood summers in Scotland; an imitation of Macpherson's *Ossian*, "The Death of Calmar and Orla"; and a lengthy ballad, "Oscar of Alva," suggested by the story from Friedrich von Schiller.

Indicative of a major interest and admiration of the young poet is his imitation of Augustan satire, "On a Change of Masters at a Great Public School," in which, following the example of his admired master Pope, he strives to achieve in heroic couplets something of the polished, disciplined satire of the great Augustan:

> Where are those honours, IDA! once your own,
> When Probus fill'd your magisterial throne?
> As ancient Rome, fast falling to disgrace,
> Hail'd a Barbarian in her Caesar's place,
> So you, degenerate, share as hard a fate,
> And seat *Pomposus* where your *Probus* sate.
> Of narrow brain, yet of a narrower soul,
> Pomposus holds you in his harsh controul....

These predominantly sentimental and imitative early verses are accompanied by several realistic and mildly cynical poems and some that are openly erotic. One of the second category is "To Mary" which had appeared in his earlier, privately printed *Fugitive Pieces,* and which had become one of the casualties of his collection when Byron destroyed it to please his serious advisers. Typical of the lines that disturbed the Reverend Becher are the following:

> Now, by my soul, 'tis most delight
> To view each other panting, dying,
> In love's *extatic posture* lying,
> Grateful to *feeling,* as to *sight.*

A second poem to Mary, "To Mary, On Receiving Her Picture," still amorous but more acceptably sentimental, passed muster with the poet's conventional Southwell friends.

Prophetic of one of the major characteristics of Byron's mature poetry is the witty, realistic treatment of false sentiment in "To a Lady Who Presented the Author a Lock of Hair, Braided with his Own, and Appointed a Night in December to Meet Him in the Garden":

> Why should you weep, like *Lydia Languish,*
> And fret with self-created anguish?   5 1-2
> Or doom the lover you have chosen,
> On winter nights to sigh half frozen;
> In leafless shades, to sue for pardon,
> Only because the scene's a garden?
>
> . . . .
>
> Think on our silly situation,
> And curb this rage for imitation . . .

Clearly, these lines are early foreshadowings of the humor and realism of the *Don Juan* manner. As Calvert has said of the budding poet, "He is already a contradictory and interesting spirit."[5] But most of these promising elements of eroticism, realism, and satire were reluctantly sacrificed by the author at the urging of his circumspect friends. Thus, imitative and sentimental, and preceded by an apologetic Preface pleading youthful inexperience and disclaiming any serious interest in a poetic career, *Hours of Idleness* was a sitting duck for hostile reviewers.

Although *Hours of Idleness* was at first reviewed favorably in a few of the lesser magazines, it was severely ridiculed in the fall number of *The Satirist* by Hewson Clarke. Byron retaliated by including Clarke among the objects of his personal "Dunciad" — "British Bards" — that was modeled after Pope and Gifford and that he was then engaged in writing.

II *Nobleman Author*

Buoyed by personal pride in his new status as a noble bard and by an advancement on his allowance adequate to clear his debts, Byron returned to Cambridge late in June in high spirits and with such change in his appearance from his thinning regimen that he was scarcely recognized by his intimates. He renewed his attachment to his protégé, John Edleston, the Trinity choir boy, and soon was drawn into a Cambridge circle of young intellectuals and political liberals with whom he formed some of his most lasting friendships. Among these were John Cam Hobhouse, a widely read youth with literary and political ambitions and with liberal Whig leanings; Charles Skinner Matthews, a gay and profane mischief-maker; Scrope Davies, already well-known in the London salons and gaming-rooms as a crony of Beau Brummell; and Francis Hodgson, an earnest, conventional young Classical scholar and tutor at King's College.

One of Byron's unconventionalities at Cambridge was keeping a pet bear in the small tower room above his spacious quarters in Merton-hall Corner of the Great Court of Trinity College. Byron proposed to the discomfited authorities that the bear "should *sit for a fellowship*."[6] However, the bear was eventually expelled from the university for misconduct and his master shipped him off to Newstead. But bruin's academic stint is still remembered at Cambridge, as I learned when I inquired, in the summer of 1964, regarding the location of Byron's rooms at Trinity. "Who cares where Lord Byron lived?" replied a glum-faced lounger in the porter's office with a fierce mustache, bowler hat, and Cockney accent. "Dirty old reprobate! Kept a bear in his quarters!"

When at the end of 1807 Byron left Cambridge, he took up residence in London in the new role of nobleman author and dandy. He was already toying with the idea of an Eastern tour — not the conventional Grand Tour — after his twenty-first birthday, a plan that frightened his excitable mother. In the meantime, he made visits to Harrow, enjoying immensely his status as a poet and "hero"; and he continued writing his "British Bards," all the while keeping a concerned eye on the reviews of his poems. Now, for the first time, the young lord engaged so excessively in sensual pleasure that his health was jeopardized. Among the "nymphs" supplied Byron by Gentleman Jackson was one girl who lived with the young lord disguised in boy's clothing. When the "young gentleman miscarried in a certain family hotel in Bond Street," the entire menage was thrown into a furore.[7]

In February, 1808, the young lord's "little fabric of fame" was demolished by an unwarrantedly savage and cruelly personal review of *Hours of Idleness* by Henry Brougham in the influential Whig journal, *The Edinburgh Review*. Although the review was considerably deserved, and not actually unjust, Byron was outraged, and his immediate response was to seek revenge. He said, later, that he could not rest until he had "vented my wrath and my rhyme ... against everything and everybody."[8] As M. K. Joseph correctly observes, the review benefited the young poet greatly by turning him away from sentimental, occasional verse and by providing him with a new subject and a new emotion. His new subject was contemporary poets and critics; his emotion, hatred and satiric scorn.[9] Assuming the approved Augustan role of censor and moralist, and looking back at his mentor Pope while modeling his satire largely upon William Gifford's *Baviad* and *Maeviad,* Byron poured out his wrath in a retaliatory satire, *English Bards and Scotch Reviewers,* a work in which Byron first truly found himself.

III   English Bards and Scotch Reviewers

Depressed more than he was willing to admit by the severity of the *Edinburgh* denunciation, he solaced himself with sea bathing on the Sussex coast with Hobhouse and Davies; and, after taking his master's degree at Cambridge in July, he returned to Newstead, Lord Grey having completed his tenancy. Byron's chief occupation at this period was the completing of his satire, a work he hoped to publish before he departed for the East. By the first of the year Byron was back in London, making arrangements for the publication of his satire and for taking his seat in the House of Lords. He was in fine fettle on January 22, 1809, the day he attained his majority, for he had prospects of authorship and a career in Parliament; but he was considerably rebuffed shortly after when Lord Carlisle made no effort to introduce him to the House of Lords and Byron was obliged to prove the legitimacy of his pedigree to the Chancellor before taking his seat. Belatedly, on March 13, Lord Byron made his official appearance in Parliament without benefit of introduction. Eschewing affiliation with either party, the proud young lord "carelessly seated himself for a few minutes on one of the empty benches to the left of the throne, usually occupied by the Lords in opposition."[10]

A few days later Byron's first major poetic work of his career, *English Bards and Scotch Reviewers,* was published anonymously by Cawthorn in an edition of one thousand copies. In this vigorous Popean satire in heroic couplets running to one thousand and seventy lines, Byron laid about him violently without regard to whether the blows fell on friend or foe; he attacked virtually all his contemporaries, except Samuel Rogers and Thomas Campbell, and denounced all critics as jaundiced and malicious and as "usurpers on the Throne of Taste." "A man must serve his time to every trade / Save Censure — Critics all are ready made." Scott is castigated for Medieval romancing and mercenary motives; Southey, for epic-mongering; and Wordsworth, for equating poetry and prose: "Who, both by precept and example, shows / That prose is verse, and verse is merely prose. . . ." Coleridge is ridiculed for his poetic obscurities and as "The bard who soars to elegize an ass." Moore and Lewis are accused of pandering to lust and immorality, W. L. Bowles is disparaged as a sentimentalist, and Erasmus Darwin is hailed as a "mighty master of unmeaning rhyme."

Byron then concentrates upon the Scotch reviewers, calling them "Northern Wolves, that still in darkness prowl; / A coward Brood, which mangle as they prey, / By hellish instinct, all that cross their way." He singled out for special vituperation "immortal Jeffrey" whom he mistakenly regarded as the author of the *Edinburgh* attack on his *English Bards*. Then, scorning his unworthy contemporaries, he offers Homer, Virgil, Tasso, Camoëns, Milton, Dryden, and Pope as the standards of poetry; and he calls upon Gifford, the contemporary champion of eighteenth-century Classical standards, to waken and strike his lyre. Byron promises to lay down his own pen "when some Bard in virtue strong, / Gifford perchance, shall raise the chastening song."

William Marshall, in his perceptive analysis of the structure of Byron's major poems, points out the chief structural deficiency of *English Bards and Scotch Reviewers*. He suggests that the fault can best be understood in terms of "Byron's use but final abandonment of a metaphor that should become the cohesive force in the poem, the traditional equation between priest and poet." Byron points to Pope and Dryden as exemplifying the priestly tradition, one no longer apparent among the bards and reviewers "in these degenerate days." But he never employs the metaphor consistently; since he again and again interpolates less relevant sections and passages, unity is so impaired that the poem becomes "essentially a series of sketches."[11]

But, despite its faults of technical imprecision, crude ridicule, and palpable misjudgments of his contemporaries, Byron's first major work still appeals by virtue of its vitality, youthful vigor, and occasional flashes of forceful wit. Published anonymously in the spring of 1809, the work was immediately recognized as Byron's, praised by Gifford, and accorded such acclaim that it ran through four editions. Byron had discovered, and expressed in this work, his sincere and lasting allegiance to Pope; and he continued to think well of his own personal "Dunciad" until 1812 when he suppressed a fifth edition of the satire because he now realized that he had attacked, when he was "young and curly," too many people like Scott, Moore, and Jeffrey whom he had come to respect. And, although he later regretted he had ever written his youthful diatribe, he never ceased to admire Pope and to return from time to time to the heroic couplet and the Augustan manner. Examples are the derivative *Hints from Horace; The Curse of Minerva,* attacking Lord Elgin for his "rape" of the Parthenon marbles; and the very late *Age of Bronze.*

This ambivalence points up one of the aspects that make Byron, in W. J. Calvert's words, "a contradictory and interesting spirit." In the excellent *Byron: Romantic Paradox,* one of the first of the few full-length critical studies of the poet, Calvert reminds us that the world of 1809 was on the whole a hostile one for an author of Classical principles. The very essence of the time was change, not conformity; experimentation, not authority; emotion, not reason. Revolution on the Continent, an armed world, empires made and unmade, the *ancien régime* overthrown and partially restored, the rise to power and affluence in England of the *nouveau riche* — everything tended to encourage a volatile youth to revolt. When reaction became equated with patriotism, poets of the older generation like Wordsworth and Southey sided with reaction. Younger poets, like Shelley, dared to embrace philosophical or esthetic nonconformity and innovation. In a word, the spirit of the time was Romantic.

But Byron's temperament was stronger than any *Zeitgeist.* In appealing to Classical principles, Calvert continues, the young poet was "crying out to be saved from himself," or at least from one side of his paradoxical self. "So long as he was in constant command of his creative faculties, he was classic, neoclassic to the bone. But ever his emotion, or his imagination, nourished on the Gothic romancing of the time, intruded, and his principles were forced to the wall."[12]

Byron's *estro,* his emotional drive for self-expression, usually triumphed over his Classical will power. Two kinds of poetic compositions resulted: one, represented by the reasoned *English Bards and Scotch Reviewers;* the other by the Romantic *Childe Harold* and the Eastern Tales. Byron's emotions and interests were aroused and redirected by his Eastern tour (1809 to 1811), and this shift of interests marks the end of a period in Byron's poetic career and the beginning of a new one.

CHAPTER 3

1809–1811 The Eastern Tour

WITH his vigorous retaliatory satire published, Byron was in the mood for a farewell revel at Newstead before departing for the East. Byron and his chief cronies, Hobhouse, Matthews, and Scrope Davies, enjoyed a hilarious house party including pistol-shooting, riding, sailing, feasting, and drinking. The long evenings were not without feminine diversions supplied by the housemaids. The fact that the young lord and his guests sometimes masqueraded as monks and drank wine from a silver-mounted skull-cup gave rise, later, to exaggerated folk-tales about the orgies at Newstead.

Heady news came to Byron from London that Gifford had praised his satire and that its authorship was known. On the strength of this encouragement, Byron began preparing a second edition of *English Bards and Scotch Reviewers*. Back in London in April, Byron waited impatiently for Hanson to raise the funds necessary for his departure from England. That Byron's interest in an eventual Parliamentary career was more than desultory is indicated by the fact that he attended sessions of Parliament seven times in the spring of 1809 before leaving on his Eastern tour.[1] In fact, his aims to see other peoples and lands, to broaden his insular viewpoint, and upon his return, perhaps, to put to some political use his speech-making abilities and liberal Whig leanings also indicate his genuine interest in politics. Finally, on July 2, Byron sailed from England on the Lisbon packet with Hobhouse, taking with him his valet, Fletcher, the old manservant, Joe Murray, and his handsome young page boy, Robert Rushton (the "little page" of *Childe Harold*).

I   Childe Burun

In Lisbon by mid-July, Byron was deeply impressed by the beautiful harbor, the Tagus River, and the mountains of Cintra. Shortly thereafter, Byron and Hobhouse set off on horseback across Spain to Seville.[2] The Peninsular War was in full progress and an air of excitement prevailed everywhere. They were off next to Cadiz, Hobhouse grumbling about the hardships of travel; but Byron, a cheerful "good traveler," was delighted with everything, especially the "oranges and women." At the nearby Port of Santa Maria the two young Englishmen witnessed a bullfight which so repelled yet fascinated Byron that he later devoted a dozen stanzas of *Childe Harold* to it. From Gibraltar, Byron sent Murray and young Rushton back to England as unfit for rigorous travel.

Byron was exhilarated as the brig *Spider* entered the Ionian Sea and approached Greece. Sailing between Cephalonia and Zante, the ship anchored briefly at Patras, behind which rose the mountains of the Peloponnesus; then it proceeded toward Prevesa. Enroute, Byron passed by the town of Missolonghi where fifteen years later he was to die in the cause of Greek independence. On October 1 Byron and Hobhouse, bound for Jannina, set out from Prevesa with a Greek guide and their retinue. Traveling sometimes by boat, sometimes on horseback, they made slow progress by way of Salora and Arta; they were entertained one night by Albanian soldiers who sang Albanian and Greek songs. In Oriental-looking Jannina, with its domes and minarets rising among orange and lemon groves above the lake, they were royally entertained by representatives of Ali Pasha. Here Byron bought several magnificent Albanian costumes which he later delighted in wearing.

A week's journey through savage scenery, which reminded Byron of the Scottish Highlands, and through severe lightning and thunderstorms brought them to Tepelene, Ali Pasha's capital. Entertained by the Eastern potentate in the sumptuous, barbaric splendor of his miniature Oriental court in this remote region of the Epirus, Byron was in seventh heaven. The experience had an Arabian Nights quality which the romantic English lord never forgot and which he later celebrated vividly in his travel-poem, *Childe Harold*. The Ali Pasha, sophisticated, sensuous, luxury-loving, ruthless, and cruel, was the type of "noble villain" Byron was to portray in his Eastern tales and represent as Haidée's "piratical papa," Lambro, in *Don Juan*.[3] Back in Jannina, Byron, eager to record his exciting experiences, read a selection from Spenser's *Faerie Queene* and was impressed with the suitability of the Spenserian stanza for a poetic travelogue. On October 31, 1809, he began writing the first canto of *Childe Harold's Pilgrimage*, which he originally called *Childe Burun* (an old form of his own name). The first canto he completed at Athens at the end of the year; the second, at Smyrna in March, 1810.

The problem now was to get from Prevesa to Patras. When Byron and Hobhouse accepted Ali Pasha's offer of an armed Turkish ship, an attempted sea voyage ensued that had all the characteristics of an *opéra bouffe* farce. Unaware that the Turks were notoriously poor sailors, Byron and Hobhouse embarked November 8 on the galiot with a crew of thirty-six Turks and four Greeks. The ship encountered a mild storm, the Turkish crew panicked, the captain threw up his hands and went below decks to await his fate, and the four Greeks managed to get the ship back into a bay north of Prevesa. Byron, unperturbed throughout, was hugely amused.

Byron and Hobhouse then made their way to Prevesa by land and from there, with thirty-seven Albanian soldiers as a bodyguard, began their six-day journey overland through the robberinfested wilderness of Acarnania to Missolonghi. Byron found the whole experience exhilarating, and he especially enjoyed the romantic nightly spectacle of the picturesquely clad Albanian soldiers, who wildly danced around the campfires and sang their barbaric songs.[4] This Albanian adventure was the very stuff of romance for his *Childe Harold*.

Back at fateful Missolonghi, Byron and Hobhouse sailed to Patras where they rested among the orange and olive groves from their arduous journey through the forests of Acarnania. Instead of proceeding through Corinth to Athens, they yielded to the allure of distant Mount Parnassus and crossed the Gulf of Corinth to Salona, from which they visited Delphi and gazed with awe upon the mountains of the gods. Byron was inspired to switch, in his *Pilgrimage* poem, from celebrating Spain to paying tribute to the home of Apollo and the Muses.

II *Byron in Athens*

The English travelers, who then began their journey on horse-back to Athens, traveled by Thebes to Scourta, where they spent a dreary Christmas Eve. Next day Byron had his first thrilling view of Athens from a rocky hilltop north of the city which he later described: "Athens, Pentilicus, Hymettus, the Aegean, and the Acropolis, burst upon the eye at once."[5] The party rode into Athens on the evening of Christmas Day and found lodging in Hagia Street at the foot of the Acropolis in the house of Mrs. Tarsia Macri, a widow with three daughters. Byron was soon attracted to the lovely girls, Mariana, Katinka, and Theresa, all under fifteen — and especially to the youngest, Theresa, whom he was to celebrate as the "Maid of Athens."

While Hobhouse explored the small, unprepossessing town within its circling walls, Byron met and enjoyed a friendly relationship with Giovanni Lusieri, the Italian landscape painter and topographical draftsman who was employed by Lord Elgin to superintend the removal and shipment to England of statues and friezes from the Acropolis. Soon Byron was thoroughly enjoying life in this sun-filled land. He rode to Eleusis, Pentelicus, and Hymettus, or down to Piraeus to bathe in the sea; visited with Lusieri; joined in the congenial social affairs; and admired the Macri sisters. When he first visited the Acropolis on January 8, 1810, he was awed by the ancient grandeur but depressed by the quiescence of the modern Greeks under the degrading oppression of Turkish rule.

His indignation at the British ravishment of Greek Classical treasures grew apace and led him to express it vehemently in the prologue of Canto II of *Childe Harold*. Byron's angry protest against Lord Elgin's "rape" of Greek treasures had far-reaching and influential effects. As Sir Steven Runciman has recently pointed out, although the Shirley brothers — Anthony, Thomas, and Robert — of the early seventeenth century were the first British Philhellenes to anticipate the Byronic tradition, Lord Byron first vividly expressed and widely disseminated a realistic awareness of modern Greece and its qualities. Lord Byron, both by poetry and personal example, dramatized Philhellenism.[6]

By mid-January Byron, who had visited all the chief Classical sites of Athens and the vicinity, was ready to visit with Hobhouse the more remote attractions of Attica. They journeyed on horse-

back to Cape Sounion, forty miles southeast of Athens, where the
tip of Attica juts out in a great rocky headland into the Aegean Sea.
Here, high on the edge of the cliff, stood the Temple of Poseidon
(then thought to be that of Minerva), its Doric columns gleaming
white against the blue sky. From this height, overlooking the deep-
blue Aegean, Byron beheld the green islands of the Cyclades, "The
Isles of Greece," which he was later to celebrate in *Don Juan,*
Canto III:

> The Isles of Greece, the Isles of Greece!
>   Where burning Sappho loved and sung,
> Where grew the arts of War and Peace,
>   Where Delos rose, and Phoebus sprung!
> Eternal summer gilds them yet,   5
> But all, except their Sun, is set.

The next day the travelers rode northward along the eastern
shore of Attica to the plain of Marathon, where Byron was moved
to further thoughts about the contrast between the glorious past
and ignominious present of Greece. This occasion was the inspiration of what became perhaps the most quoted of all Byron's lines
(vying with his famous "Apostrophe to the Ocean") — lines which
effectively "fired Greek nationalist pride and spurred Philhellenic
zeal":[7]

> The mountains look on Marathon —   5
>   And Marathon looks on the sea;
> And musing there an hour alone,
>   I dreamed that Greece might still be free;
> For standing on the Persians' grave,
> I could not deem myself a slave.

On March 5 came the opportunity to continue the Eastern tour
on the English sloop, *Pylades,* bound for Smyrna. Eager to see the
Near East but reluctant to leave congenial Athens, Byron, with
Hobhouse, nonetheless made an abrupt departure. Byron was sad
at leaving behind two persons for whom he had formed romantic
attachments typical of his ambivalent idealizations of beautiful
youths and maidens. One was Nicolo Giraud, a handsome sixteen-
year-old youth of French descent and a kinsman of Lusieri. The

other was Theresa Macri, to whom Byron addressed the famous lines:

> Maid of Athens, ere we part,
> Give, oh give me back my heart!
> . . . .
> Hear my vow before I go,
> *Zoe mou, sas agapo.*   7 1-2

The tender refrain, "My soul, I love you," must have haunted the romantic young poet as he sailed away.

Arriving at Smyrna on March 8, Byron and Hobhouse first visited the ruins of Ephesus, then returned to Smyrna, where Byron occupied himself with describing in *Childe Harold* his wildly romantic adventures in Albania. He then depicted his impressions of and thoughts about Greece, especially stressing the desperate need of the modern Greeks for courageous self-reliance:

> When riseth Lacedemon's Hardihood,
> When Thebes' Epaminondas rears again,   5
> When Athens' children are with hearts endued,
> When Grecian mothers shall give birth to men,
> Then may'st thou be restored; but not till then.

With this challenge Byron concluded the second canto of *Childe Harold* and put the manuscript about his travels away in his trunk.

Aboard the frigate *Salsette* in early April, Byron and his companion sailed northward beside the island of Lesbos and approached the Hellespont. While the ship was becalmed off Cape Janissary, the young men explored the "ringing plains of windy Troy" and gazed at distant Mount Ida. Although Byron was deeply moved by the Homeric scenes, an even more exciting opportunity challenged the athletic poet. Accompanied by Mr. Ekenhead, a lieutenant from the *Salsette,* Byron set out to imitate Leander's famous achievement. On May 3 Byron swam the Hellespont, from Sestos to Abydos, in one hour and ten minutes. The actual distance is one mile, but the strong tide lengthened the swim to four miles. Shortly after the event, Byron penned his gay lines, "Written After Swimming From Sestos to Abydos."

The wind favoring the *Salsette* finally made its way through the straits and anchored on May 13 at Constantinople. The magnificence of the city with its domes and minarets and cypresses was not lost on the wide-eyed poet, nor was the Oriental splendor of the Seraglio and the luxuriant springtime beauty of the adjacent gardens along the Golden Horn and Bosporus. Dramatic contrasts of squalor and Turkish brutality heightened the experience. A notable event of Byron's stay in Constantinople was his audience with the Grand Signor of Turkey in his Arabian Nights palace. Much later Byron was to be allied with the Greeks against the Grand Signor in their struggle for independence.

In Athens again by mid-July, Byron was pleasantly situated in the Capuchin convent (actually a Franciscan monastery) at the foot of the Acropolis. He found this semi-hostelry, with its assortment of congenial companions and gay buffooneries, altogether pleasant. Much as he appreciated his friend Hobhouse, who had returned to England, he was more relaxed and uninhibited with no fellow Englishman about. His favorite pastime was swimming with his handsome youthful protégé, Nicolo Giraud, or sitting with him on some secluded rock above the sea.[8] One day, while thus daydreaming near Piraeus, Byron spied a strange procession moving toward the sea. Inquiry revealed it to be a handful of soldiers bent upon executing a Turkish girl who had been taken in the act of illicit love: sewed into a sack, she was to be thrown into the sea. Byron ordered the soldiers, at pistol point, to return the girl to the Waiwode (Turkish governor) of Athens. After Byron had persuaded this official to release the girl, on condition that she leave Athens, he helped her to escape to Thebes. This episode later provided Byron with the situation which he employed in his first Oriental tale, *The Giaour.*[9]

Byron's fall and winter in Athens were, for the most part, spent pleasantly; for the sociable and much-admired young English lord participated in the lively activities of Athenian society and found the cosmopolitan community intellectually stimulating. On his second visit to Sounion, Byron carved his name on the square column of the Temple of Poseidon where Greeks today point to it with pride. While residing in the "far from ecclesiastical monastery," Byron also studied Armenian, Italian, and modern Greek. And for recreation there were a number of compliant young ladies in Athens, as well as Nicolo Giraud.

In March Byron's increased rancor against Lord Elgin as the

saboteur of Greece burst forth in a vitriolic satire, *The Curse of Minerva,* in which he represented Minerva as placing an eternal curse on Elgin for his rape of her land. Ironically enough, when Byron took his reluctant leave of Athens on April 22, 1811, the poet with his manuscript of the *Curse of Minerva* found himself on board the transport ship *Hydra* which carried in its cargo a large shipment of the Elgin Marbles.

Placing Nicolo Giraud in school at Malta, Byron sailed for England on June 2 on board the frigate *Volage.* He arrived in Sheerness on July 14, something over two years since he had left England. Although Lord Byron returned home outwardly the same, inwardly he had matured into a genuine cosmopolite with liberalized political views and with a clarified vision of the prejudices and predilections of insular England.

III   *Byron in England Again*

Byron was welcomed home by Hobhouse and Scrope Davies, as well as by Dallas, his literary agent, who had heard that the poet was bringing home a new manuscript. Byron produced it casually as of little importance, but Dallas was enthusiastic about *Childe Harold* and eager to get it published, although he urged the toning down of passages expressing unorthodox views of religion and politics. Although Byron refused to make such revisions, Dallas set about finding a publisher. Fortunately, he soon interested John Murray II, who enjoyed a high reputation as the publisher of Scott, Southey, and Gifford, and who was already favorably predisposed toward the young author of the successful *English Bards and Scotch Reviewers.*

Murray agreed to publish *Childe Harold,* and Byron reluctantly consented to the publisher's desire to have the author's name appear on the title page. Byron's concern was not so much fear of public disapproval of his liberal views as of critical reaction to the sentimental tone of the poem and to its self-revelation. Strongly desirous of not being identified with Harold, the hero of the *Pilgrimage,* Byron insisted in his Preface on the entirely fictitious nature of his principal character. But, when he stubbornly refused to alter or delete verses expressing his skeptical views on religion and immortality, he declared thus early the intense despite for hypocrisy, religious or political, which characterized him through-

out his life. For the motto of *Childe Harold* he chose a sentence
from *Le Cosmopolite, ou, le Citoyen du Monde* of Fougeret de
Monbron which succinctly captured the noble poet's new-found
sense of cosmopolitanism: *"L'univers est une espèce de livre, dont
on n'a lu que la première page quand on n'a vue que son pays."*[10]

On August 1 came word of his mother's critical illness and the
next day the stunning news of her death. Alone at Newstead, the
young lord's grief for his erratic and unworthy yet doting mother
was genuine: "I had but one friend in the world, and she is
gone!"[11] Within a few days of his mother's death, news came of the
death of two of Byron's best friends, Charles Skinner Matthews,
his brilliant Cambridge associate, and John Wingfield, his Harrow
schoolfellow. Heavy with thoughts of mortality, Byron drew up a
will in which he made Hobhouse and Davies his executors and in
which he left seven thousand pounds to Nicolo Giraud on the
attainment of his majority, and Newstead to his cousin, George
Byron.

In October Byron learned belatedly of the death the previous
May of John Edleston, the former choir boy of Trinity. Edleston
was one, he wrote, "whom I loved more than I ever loved a living
thing..."[12] Deeply moved, Byron expressed his sorrow in the poem
"To Thyrza," deliberately using a girl's name to conceal the identity of his lost friend from the public, although not from such an
intimate as Hobhouse. This was the first of several "Thyrza"
poems Byron was to write. He also added stanzas to Edleston in
Childe Harold.[13]

Byron's friendship with Thomas Moore began through a challenge that fizzled. Offended by Byron's jibe in *English Bards,*
Moore had attempted to call the young lord to account. Upon
Byron's return to England, the Irish poet was mollified by Byron's
disarming explanation; and the two poets met in November at
dinner in the home of their mutual friend, Samuel Rogers, the
banker-poet. Byron's ingratiating charm completely won Moore,
and thereafter the two were on the best terms, Moore eventually
becoming Byron's biographer. Byron was very much pleased to
associate on equal terms with those he regarded as the "first" literary men of England of his day: Thomas Moore, Samuel Rogers,
and Thomas Campbell. Byron's first personal contact with Coleridge occurred in December when upon two occasions he accom-

panied Rogers to hear Coleridge, "who is a kind of rage at present," lecture on Shakespeare.[14]

Before Christmas Byron went to Newstead with two of his Cambridge friends, Francis Hodgson and William Harness, who were made uneasy by the rioting of the "frame-breakers" (weavers) at nearby Nottingham. Later, this event supplied Byron with ammunition for his maiden speech in Parliament. In the meantime, he was touching up the proofs of *Childe Harold* and in the evenings taking his recreation with the three pretty housemaids of his Newstead "seraglio" of whom his favorite was Susan Vaughan. And so 1811 ended quietly.

CHAPTER 4

1812–1815 Childe Harold *I–II* and Sudden Fame

IN mid-January 1812 Byron resumed his seat in the House of Lords. His Harrow-days ambition of oratory and politics had returned. During the six sessions he attended in January he was looking for a cause to ally himself with and casting about for a subject for his maiden speech. No major issues were under debate at the moment. George III (Shelley's "... old, mad, blind, despised, and dying king") had been replaced by the Prince Regent who, by deserting his Whig friends, made it impossible for them to form a government. This rebuff spurred all Whigs to unite in opposition to the reactionary Tories. Byron did not wish to ally himself with the Radical leaders in Parliament but to work with the Liberal Whigs represented by Lord Holland.[1]

I *Byron in Politics*

By early February Byron had decided to speak in behalf of the unemployed weavers of Nottingham. Displaced by improvements in weaving machinery, the unemployed workers had begun breaking frames in November, 1811. When efforts of militia to quell the violence in December and January were unavailing, the only remedy proposed by the oppressive Tory government under the leadership of Lord Chancellor Eldon was to increase the severity of punishment for frame-breaking, Accordingly, the Tory riot-bill that provided the death-penalty for frame-breaking was introduced in the House of Commons in mid-February and was passed on February 20.

Eschewing all caution, Lord Byron made a frontal attack on the Frame Bill in his maiden speech in the House of Lords on February

27. He denounced the ruthlessness and injustice of the bill and made an eloquent appeal for "the industrious poor" on humanitarian principles. For the unemployed and starving frame-breaker the only succor proposed by the government was that "new capital punishments must be devised, new snares of death must be spread for the wretched mechanic, who is famished into guilt."[2] Complimented upon his address by Lord Holland and other Moderate Whigs, and replied to by Lord Chancellor Eldon, Byron felt encouraged in his debut in "Opposition." Toward the end of his life he was to declare in *Don Juan* (XV, 22) "I was born for opposition." The young lord now had the satisfaction of sitting on the committee that modified the Frame Bill penalty from death to fine or imprisonment.[3]

On the threshold of an auspicious Parliamentary career and already recognized as a formidable satirist, Lord Byron was suddenly diverted from both politics and satire by the publication of *Childe Harold*. A few days after its appearance on March 10, Byron wrote: "I awoke one morning and found myself famous."[4] Not only at Holland House, the social and literary mecca of London society, but in all the drawing-rooms of Whig aristocracy the young nobleman-poet was sought after and lionized. Shy in society and studiedly self-possessed, the handsome, youthful Lord Byron was immediately identified with Harold, the melancholy and cynical hero of the romantic *Childe Harold's Pilgrimage*.

Receiving the admiration of many fashionable women, and discussed at all dinner tables, Byron was soon enmeshed in an affair with the vivacious and eccentric Lady Caroline Lamb, who besieged him with her attentions. He was fascinated by the impulsive Caroline, the first woman of his own rank and intellect to attract him romantically; and soon his infatuation was interfering with his "senatorial duties." Although he continued a desultory attendance at Parliamentary sessions, Byron spoke only twice more in the House of Lords: On April 21, 1812, on the Catholic Claims Bill; and on June 1, 1813, when he presented Cartwright's petition for reform of Parliament.[5] Thus the acclaim of *Childe Harold* and the tempestuous Caroline Lamb affair eclipsed the young lord's Parliamentary career at its auspicious beginning.

Best evidence of the literary acceptance of Lord Byron was the laudatory review of *Childe Harold* in the *Edinburgh Review* in early May. Byron promptly apologized to Jeffrey for his attack in

English Bards and Scotch Reviewers, and Jeffrey replied very graciously.[6] In the same repentant mood Byron wrote Sir Walter Scott an apology for his unjust remarks in *English Bards.* This overture was the beginning of a cordial, enduring personal friendship between the two poets.

II   Childe Harold *I–II*

Byron's two-year Eastern tour, from the summer of 1809 to the summer of 1811, had supplied the impressionable young lord from insular England with new horizons, interests, and emotions. The strange world of the Levant, especially the wilds of Albania, provided some of the most vivid experiences of his life.[7] The Arabian Nights splendor of Ali Pasha's feudal court at Tepelene, combined with vivid memories of Scott's metrical romances, supplied the immediate impetus for commencing the composition of *Childe Harold's Pilgrimage.* The original suggestion of such a poem may have been made to Byron by John Galt on board ship from Malta to Greece. But the analogues are numerous among the eighteenth-century landscape and travel-poems of such authors as James Thomson, William Shenstone, James Beattie, and Oliver Goldsmith. The poem eventually bears resemblance to a poetical diary of Byron's vivid poetic impressions of people and places. Whatever unity the work possesses is one of tone, not structure. And the tone is achieved in the conception of Harold, the original "Byronic hero," and in the strength and verve of the poetry by which he is presented.

In Canto I, Byron introduces his hero, Harold, and then takes him on his "Pilgrimage," first to Lisbon and Cintra and thence across Spain, where the Peninsular War is in progress, to Cadiz, where Harold is charmed by Spanish women and love and where he witnesses a bullfight. This canto, with its pseudo-medieval, fictitious framework and occasional flashes of vivid description, concludes with serious reflections on the servile status of the Spanish nation. Canto II, more unified, opens with a meditation on the Acropolis and closes, in its original form (before the poet's addition of accretive stanzas), with a meditation on Greek freedom. Within this framework, the substance of the canto is mainly Byron's romantic Albanian adventure. The deletions Byron made from the two cantos — a considerable number of burlesque and

satiric passages unacceptable to his literary advisers in London —
point ahead to the serio-comic mode which later characterized *Don
Juan.*[8]

For all these new experiences and feelings Byron needed a newer,
more flexible stanzaic medium than any he had heretofore employed. The heroic couplet he had exploited in *English Bards and
Scotch Reviewers* to the limits of his ability. He realized that he had
nothing more to say in conventional satire. Almost fortuitously he
came upon the right form for his new departure in verse. As noted
earlier, Byron had read a selection from Spenser's *Faerie Queene* in
Jannina, and had been impressed with the suitability of the Spenserian stanza for a poetic travelogue; but for his use of this meter,
Byron looked to James Beattie's *The Minstrel* and to other
eighteenth-century Spenserians, such as Thomson and Shenstone,
rather than to Spenser himself. All these, not without precedent in
Spenser, had exploited the meter for a wide variety of effects, including description, sentiment, satire, burlesque, and humor. With
this in mind, Byron introduced a variety of moods, including the
comic and satiric, into the original draft of *Childe Harold,* especially in the first canto, in which such elements bulked large before
his friends persuaded him to cancel them. And, although he continued to use the Spenserian stanza with effectiveness in the later
cantos of *Childe Harold,* it took another ten years of experimenting
before he found in Italian *ottava rima* the stanza form most suitable to his genius.[9]

Harold, the first of a series of Byron's "Byronic heroes," is, in
Byron's words, "a fictitious character ... introduced for the sake
of giving some connection to the piece.... Harold is the child of
imagination."[10] As has been noted, Byron's purpose was to disso-
ciate himself from the character of his poem; but his readers never
accepted the separation, no matter how much he asserted it. There
was enough likeness between Harold and Byron to warrant the
equation.

As a matter of fact, there are two central characters in the work,
the titular hero and the narrator. The former adumbrates Byron's
occasional moods of melancholy, gloom, boredom, loneliness and
disillusion; the latter reflects his more characteristic and attractive
personality. All Byron's intimates were aware of these contradictory aspects of his character: of his perplexing shifts from gloom to
gaiety, misanthropy to sociability, enthusiasm to boredom and

cynicism. But recently, Andrew Rutherford, in his penetrating and sustained critical analysis of Byron's work, has recognized the presence of this crucial dichotomy throughout Byron's poetry from beginning to end. Byron, he tells us, made an earnest, though unsuccessful, effort in the first two cantos of *Childe Harold* to establish a dramatic tension between the two separate entities of the titular hero and the narrator which might allow him to give complete expression to his own complex nature.[11] Byron did not succeed in this rudimentary attempt because, at the time, he did not realize the potential importance of the two characters. He failed "to establish any significant relationship between them; therefore, they co-exist but do not interact. The one is not observed and criticised by the other (as in *Don Juan*)."[12]

But the very fact of Byron's attempt, of his search for a proper medium to reflect the diversities of his own many-faceted character, does point hopefully forward, as Rutherford notes, to the freedom which he later found in *ottava rima* and the *Don Juan* mode. Moreover, M. K. Joseph, in his comprehensive and closely analyzed general critical study of Byron's poetry, pursues the fascinating record of Byron's quest for a mode and a technique that would allow him freedom to express the paradoxical diversities of his nature and, at the same time, stand aside and comment upon his experiences with sympathetic detachment. In *Childe Harold,* Joseph remarks, "Byron is already moving towards the separation of hero and narrator which was to become, later, the master-device of *Don Juan*."[13]

One of Byron's occasional moods — and a role his avid readers virtually insisted that he assume — was that of melancholy misanthrope. Just as Harold takes on the attributes now of Cain, the Wandering Jew, the Gothic novel hero-villain, Rousseauistic Child of Nature, "Gloomy Egoist," and Man of Feeling (as Peter L. Thorslev thoroughly analyzes in his full-length study of the Byronic hero),[14] so Byron was expected to possess the attributes of his hero. And, although he vehemently maintained that he "would not be such a fellow," he was everywhere regarded less as a poet than as a mysterious romantic figure, satiated and secretly wicked, but magnetically attractive. As Calvert comments, had Byron more thoroughly differentiated his hero and his narrator, he would not have been obliged to protest the popular equation so much. "For the next four years his life is the disastrous result of playing up to the popular conception of him.''[15]

However, on the credit side of the ledger, there is in the earlier *Childe Harold* the beginning of another Byronic method which he later uses masterfully in *Don Juan*. This is the achievement of moral comment through the blending of narrative with digression, satiric or otherwise. We have already noted Byron's use in Canto II of the meditation on the Acropolis as a framework for the Albanian adventure. Closely related to this developing virtue of meditative digression is Byron's growing sense of structure. Byron always needs *lebensraum* in which to gain his effects. Graham Hough's observation is correct: ''The sweep of a whole canto of *Childe Harold* or *Don Juan* is needed before we can see what he is at.''[16] Although we have to wait for *Don Juan* to meet with the expert balancing of structure and detail, evidences of Byron's coming capacity are apparent already.

Childe Harold, then, beginning perhaps as the projection of a Byronic attitude in the shape of a central figure, becomes substantially altered as the descriptive-meditative elements increase during the course of the first two cantos and as the importance of the titular hero diminishes. Even before Byron writes Canto IV, he has given up the futile effort to keep his titular hero separate from the narrator. And, as Rutherford remarks, Byron in writing *in propria persona* and in giving us his impressions of countries, peoples, scenes, and incidents from his own tour succeeds in interesting the modern reader far more with his vivid travelogue than with the ruminations of his lugubrious Harold. ''One is conscious of an interesting mind and personality at work here.''[17] *Childe Harold* I–II, with Byron's revisions, writes Jerome J. McGann, changed from a ''personal travelogue'' to ''the revolutionary confessional poem which so decisively influenced Romantic and post-Romantic art.''[18]

Childe Harold as a meditative poem, with antecedents in the eighteenth-century topographical-meditative mode as well as in the ''ruins of time'' meditative tradition of Classical Latin poetry, is the subject of Joseph's fascinating account of the topographical tradition.[19] This tradition, which can be traced as far back as Virgil, Horace, and Ovid, has its modern equivalents in such poems as William Butler Yeats' ''The Wild Swans at Coole.'' In England, John Denham's *Cooper's Hill* revived the form which was admired and imitated by Alexander Pope, James Thomson, John Dyer, and many others in the eighteenth century. An integral ingredient of this genre, as practiced by Denham and the eighteenth-century writers, is moral reflection on the scene or subject. The habit of moralizing on the scenes which he describes is a characteristic of Byron which in *Childe Harold* is attributed both to Harold and to the narrator, but predominantly to the latter.

Examples of the coupling of topographical description with moralistic reflection abound in Cantos I and II. Particularly telling are the thoughts evoked by the ruins of Classic Greece:

> Fair Greece! sad relic of departed Worth!
> Immortal, though no more; though fallen, great!   3
> Who now shall lead thy scattered children forth,
> And long accustomed bondage uncreate?
> Not such thy sons who whilome did await,
> The hopeless warriors of a willing doom,
> In bleak Thermopylae's sepulchral strait —
> Oh! who that gallant spirit shall resume,
> Leap from Eurota's banks, and call thee from the tomb?
>   (II, lxxiii)

And answering his own question, Byron continues:

> When riseth Lacedemon's Hardihood,
> When Thebes' Epaminondas rears again,
> When Athens' children are with hearts endued,
> When Grecian mothers shall give birth to men,
> Then may'st thou be restored; but not till then. . . .
>   (II, lxxxiv)

If, then, *Childe Harold* as a topographical-meditative poem was part of a well-established and ongoing tradition, how account for its unparalleled popular reception and wide acclaim? Was Byron's interest in the Levant unique?

As Joseph reminds us, with the Continent closed to travel by the Napoleonic wars, the Levant was a natural mecca for sightseers, antiquarians, archaeologists, artists, and litterateurs — the "Levant lunatics." "Byron was aware that the ground was prepared for him and *Childe Harold* II is, in a way, the culmination of a process."[20] The widespread interest, especially in Greece and her past glory, and the speculation over the possibility of a national resurgence and overthrow of Turkish domination formed the background of Byron's own interest, his characteristic attitudes, and his utterances.

Nor was the writing of poetry about contemporary Greece something brand new. There was, for example, William Falconer's *Shipwreck* of seventy years earlier, with its panorama of Greece. Terence Spencer calls this "the first elaborate treatment of modern Greece in English poetry."[21] But this and a dozen "puny predecessors" were, in Joseph's succinct words, "eclipsed forever by the sudden glory of *Childe Harold.* In the matter of Greece, Byron was simply doing very much better what others had attempted already."[22]

What was unique with Byron was his vivid description of that unknown land, Albania. Byron was virtually the first Englishman to visit it and to describe authentically the wild scenery, the half-savage Suliotes, the mountain fastnesses, and the exotic court of the tyrannical Ali Pasha. In Tepelene he sees

> The wild Albanian kirtled to his knee,
> With shawl-girt head and ornamented gun,   5 1-2
> And gold-embroidered garments, fair to see;
> The crimson-scarféd men of Macedon.

And unforgettable is his description of his picturesquely clad Suliote soldier friends escorting him through the Arcarnanian wilderness, and wildly dancing and singing around the campfires at night:

> On the smooth shore the night-fires brightly blazed,
> The feast was done, the red wine circling fast,
> . . . .
> For ere night's midmost, stillest hour was past,   2 1-2
> The native revels of the troop began;
> Each Palikar his sabre from him cast,
> And bounding hand in hand, man linked to man,
> Yelling their uncouth dirge, long daunced the kirtled clan.

Such was the manuscript Byron brought back to England in 1811 at the bottom of his trunk, and produced reluctantly, as of dubious worth, only when his friends persuaded him. He thought more highly of his satires, two more of which, in the *English Bards* manner, he had written in Greece, *Hints from Horace* and *The Curse of Minerva*. But it was *Childe Harold* that gained him fame.

CHAPTER 5

1813–1816 Eastern Tales and Marriage

AMONG the important friends Byron made during the years of 1813–1816 were three women distinguished in London society for beauty, intellect, and influence — Lady Jersey, Lady Melbourne, and Lady Oxford. A devoted patron of the Reform movement, the beautiful and unconventional Lady Oxford interested herself in the handsome literary idol of the day with Liberal Whig leanings who seemed on the verge of a successful Parliamentary career. Perhaps recommended by her former lover, Sir Francis Burdett, Byron was elected to membership in the London Hampden Club, a Reform club of liberal aristocrats and miscellaneous Reformers. Although Lady Oxford sought to revive Byron's flagging interest in Parliament, the relationship between her and Byron was before long something other than political. During an idyllic interlude at the lovely lady's country place of Eywood the twenty-four-year-old lord was captivated by the "autumnal charms" of Lady Oxford, sixteen years his senior. Caroline Lamb, with whom Byron had been making every effort to break off, revenged herself by burning Byron in effigy.

When Byron had first met Miss Annabella Milbanke in March, he had been only casually interested in the precocious, serious-minded "bluestocking" from Seaham. But, by September, feeling that marriage would be the only escape from the toils of Caroline Lamb, Byron made a proposal to Miss Milbanke through Lady Melbourne. Nothing could better reveal Annabella's cautious, deliberate temperament than the fact that she calmly declined the offer of marriage from the most adulated, sought-after young man in London society because she could not feel a sufficiently "strong affection" for him. With good nature, and probable relief, Byron accepted the refusal, thanking Lady Melbourne for her efforts with "the amiable *Mathematician*" and "Princess of Parallelograms."[1]

Early in 1813 Byron attended Parliament several times at the urging of Lady Oxford, but he was indifferent about his "senatorial duties" and his Whig associates. Actually, Byron did not give up without inward regret his Harrow School dreams of a political career in which his oratorical efforts in behalf of worthy causes might produce important social reforms. But his brief experience of practical politics had disillusioned him. The Liberal Whigs were too cautious; the Radical Reformers too extreme. Byron was genuinely for "Reform," but he had always an aristocratic distrust for "reformers," whom he regarded as demagogues or "blackguards."

Nevertheless, he did not hesitate to do the unpopular thing when, on June 1, he stood up in the House of Lords and presented Major John Cartwright's plea for the right to petition for the "Reform" of Parliament.[2] This early example of Byron's fearless championship of freedom occurred in a period of hysterical alarm and repression comparable with that which followed World War II,[3] but the speech was Lord Byron's last one in Parliament. Now he wished to follow the example of his best friend, Hobhouse, who had recently set forth on a prolonged Continental tour. The warm Mediterranean climes of his youthful "Harold" adventures were beckoning strongly.

I *Augusta Leigh*

But events in June complicated his plans for departure. Murray, with some trepidation, published on June 5, the first of Byron's Oriental tales, *The Giaour*. Byron's admirers read the new poem with avidity; and Gifford, his literary mentor, praised it at the same time that he urged him to continue *Childe Harold*. Then, in late June, began Byron's affair with his half-sister, Augusta Leigh. Augusta, who had married her cousin Colonel George Leigh in 1807, an irresponsible spendthrift and gambler, was now living at Six Mile Bottom near Cambridge with her three small daughters. Byron and Augusta had not met since before Byron's Eastern Tour. When she came to visit him in London, he wrote to Moore ". . . my sister is in town, which is a great comfort, — for, never having been much together, we are naturally more attached to each other."[4] Throughout July Byron and Augusta were seen everywhere together at balls, in drawing-rooms, and in theaters.

Marchand's explanation of the mutual attraction and unique relationship between Lord Byron and Augusta Leigh is the most discerning that has ever been advanced. Augusta, five years Byron's senior, was "soft and voluptuous in face and figure"; and, though not beautiful, she had "the handsome Byron profile and large eyes, the long lip that could curl and pout like his own," and the habit of frowning as he did. She still had the maternal interest in him she had felt when he was a charming lad and the ability to laugh at his witticisms, indulge his whims, forgive his weaknesses, understand the unhappiness of his early years with his mother, and appreciate his sensitivity to his lameness. Between the two there need be no explanations or pretensions, no inhibition or restraint. "And the consanguinity was balanced by the charm of strangeness engendered by their separate upbringing; in their formative years they had escaped the rough familiarity of the brother-sister relationship." "Instinctively they understood each other because they were Byrons."[5]

By the end of August, Byron's confidences to Lady Melbourne left very little doubt as to the nature of the "new scrape" he was in. "Byron's correspondence with Lady Melbourne," writes Marchand, "hints very strongly that he had become involved in a liaison with his half-sister, Augusta." Byron, always attracted to the new and forbidden, found this intimate relationship both fascinating and repellent. Emancipated as he now was intellectually from the "fear-inspired" religion of his childhood, he was too realistic to ignore the dangerous consequences of his actions and too sensitive to feel no remorse: "The Calvinistic sense of sin haunted his subconscious mind, a ghost that could never be completely exorcised. But that fatalistic conception of human depravity blended with his own weakness to drive him on to further violation of the inhibitions of his own mind." The extant evidence of incest between Byron and Augusta "does not amount to *legal* proof," Marchand admits; but "the circumstantial evidence in Byron's letters can not be ignored" and "certain aspects of his life and correspondence," he concludes, "can not be explained sensibly in any other terms."[6]

Oddly enough, in the midst of Byron's affair with Augusta a letter arrived from Annabella Milbanke that cautiously explored the possibility of renewing their friendship. This incident began a curious correspondence in which Byron engaged with a cool objectivity; perhaps he was thinking of marriage with Miss Milbanke as a possible escape from his present dilemma.

As usual, he found relief from the affair with Augusta in poetic expression. "All convulsions end with me in rhyme; and to solace my midnights, I have scribbled another Turkish story..." he wrote Moore in November.[7] Seeing that the public was taken with his romantic hero, Harold, Byron took the wrong course, as Andrew Rutherford perceptively observes, "turning his back on the most promising features of *Childe Harold.*"[8] Shelving the topographical-meditative mode with its sterling virtues of moralistic and satiric digression, and forgoing the opportunity provided by *Childe Harold* for the potential development of dramatic tension between protagonist and narrator, as well as for the expression of his humorous or cynical realism, Byron yielded to popular demand and went on portraying romantic heroes in a series of Eastern Tales which largely created the myth of the Byronic Hero in England and throughout Europe.

II *Eastern Tales*

Writing with incredible speed, and with consequent carelessness in structure and style, Byron finished and published six verse tales between June, 1813, and February, 1816. In what he called his "scribbling mood" he dashed off in record time the first draft of his initial Eastern tale, *The Giaour.* Encouraged by his shrewd publisher, Murray, to ride the crest of *Childe Harold's* popularity and to capitalize effectively on his recent adventures in the Levant, Byron hurriedly composed two more tales during the same year, *The Bride of Abydos* and *The Corsair.* Melodramatic as these tales are, and deliberately as they exploit a new literary field of popular appeal, they do represent a distinct advance over *Childe Harold* in narrative interest and technique.

Byron's first Oriental tale, *The Giaour,* appeared in edition after edition as Byron continued to make large additions to the text. The public, fascinated by its purple passages and by hints of "deeds without a name," insisted on identifying Byron with his gloomy, wildly romantic heroes. Based on Byron's own experience in Athens in rescuing a Turkish girl sewed up in a sack and condemned to be drowned, *The Giaour* has as its hero a figure immediately recognizable as a more striking and virile modification of the earlier Harold. In fact, the heroes of all six of these Eastern tales — the Giaour, Selim, Conrad, Lara, Hugo, and Alp — are variations of Harold: they are gloomy, misanthropic, and lonely; but, unlike him, they are intrepid, lawless, and fiercely passionate. Endowed with illicit desires, guilt, remorse, and revenge, and equipped with fictitious adventures, these outlaw-heroes play their romantic tragedies against a background of Byron's own Eastern experiences.

Incest was the theme of his second Oriental tale, *The Bride of Abydos*. Originally the lovers, Selim and Zuleika, were brother and sister; but Byron changed their consanguinity to cousinship. Here Byron treated for the first time the theme to which he was to revert again and again. That "perverse passion," he reluctantly admitted to Lady Melbourne, "was my deepest after all."[9] No matter how hard he resisted his attraction to Augusta, "he could not escape the feeling," Marchand wisely discerns, "that no woman was so comforting and satisfying to his self-esteem as Augusta, so yielding to his every wish, so sensuous and undemanding, and so motherly and protective at the same time."[10]

The Bride of Abydos, published on December 2, 1813, was immediately devoured by Byron's fans. Gifford praised it, and Murray offered Byron one thousand guineas for the *Giaour* and the *Bride*. Byron was pleased, but he was not yet willing to accept pay for his literary work. Again he was the literary idol of London, just as he had been after the appearance of *Childe Harold*. Continuing his rapid writing in December, he completed his third Oriental tale, *The Corsair,* by New Year's Day, 1814. *The Corsair* sold ten thousand copies on the day of publication and twenty-five thousand copies in seven editions in little more than a month. In Conrad, the hero, the public insisted in seeing a self-portrait of Byron, "That man of loneliness and mystery."

In all these Eastern tales, Byron was writing primarily, as of old, to relieve his feelings and out of one of his two deepest needs — the *need to write.* Like the other, his *need to love,* his compulsion to write was irresistible. He made no pretensions to skilled craftsmanship and artistic perfection. Reflecting upon the merits of his current poetic productions, he wrote: "I have lately begun to think my things have been strangely over-rated. . . . It proves my own want of judgment in publishing, and the public's in reading things, which cannot have stamina for permanent attention."[11] This dissatisfaction with the trend of his poetic work is one of the earliest and best examples of Byron's realistic self-criticism. But, since he *must* write, popular romances would serve as well as any other. Consequently, he mined the Byronic hero vein to the utmost.

III   *The Byronic Hero*

The sources of the Byronic hero are complex. He is a composite figure whose ancestry has recently been exhaustively and definitively traced by Peter Thorslev.[12] Among the several strains of contribution are Prometheus, Milton's Satan, Rousseau's and Goethe's sentimental heroes, Horace Walpole's and Ann Radcliffe's hero-villains, Friedrich von Schiller's Karl Moor, and Scott's Marmion. Essentially, the stock hero of the Gothic novel was revived and given new currency by Byron, who endowed him with the attributes of romantic melancholy, pride, solitariness, guilty passion, defiance, violent revenge, and remorse.

Other strains are contributed, as Rutherford points out, by factors in Byron's own life. From childhood he was fascinated by the extravagant and wild exploits of his ancestors, especially by the solitariness and crimes of his uncle, "the Wicked Lord" Byron. There was also his persistent sense of guilt, from whatever obscure origins in early Calvinistic training or in premature initiation into sexual experience by his nurse or homosexuality by Lord Grey, and his obsessive interest in guilt and remorse. Moreover, his sense of having been an "outsider" when he came to London, without a circle of friends among his peers, inclined him to admire men who were proud, isolated, and rebellious, exiles or outlaws from society. Closely related was his disenchantment with civilization — "that wild, Society" — and his strong attraction to the semi-barbaric, violent, and passionate aspects of the life of the East, especially as exemplified by the wildly picturesque Suliote warriors of Albania. All these elements reinforced Byron's interest in the outlaw-hero type. Thus, a wide spectrum of contributions is needed to explain the genesis of the Byronic hero.[13]

All the Byronic heroes, including those of the three verse tales which followed in 1814 and 1815 — *Lara, Parisina,* and *The Siege of Corinth* — are presented against the vivid, colorful panorama of the Levant. Byron prided himself on the authenticity and accuracy of his descriptions of Eastern life. Locales, antiquities, costumes, and customs were drawn from his personal knowledge but were augmented by the garnerings of his wide and intensive reading which included among its many riches the writings of Paul Rycaut, Vincent Mignot, Barthélemy D'Herbelot, Sir William Jones, Baron de Tott, and Lady Mary Wortley Montagu, as well as Jonathan Scott's edition of *The Arabian Nights* and George Sale's translation of the Koran. And, perhaps most influential of all, William Beckford's *Vathek* is the work from which Byron drew extensively, with grateful acknowledgement, for concrete "local color" details and for the pervasive atmosphere of Oriental romance. To all these elements, blended with the Gothic tale, Byron added the authentic material of his own experience.[14]

In all six of these Eastern tales, the hero dominates the story; the plot is definitely subordinate to the interest in character. Each of the romances represents, with variations, a preoccupation with a stock figure in a stock situation. In the first tale, the hero, the Giaour, loves Leila, wife of Hassan. Detecting her infidelity, Hassan drowns her in a sack; and the Giaour revenges her by slaying Hassan. Later, in the guise of a monk, the guilt and remorse-ridden hero confesses and dies.

This pattern of illicit passion, death, revenge, and remorse prevails, substantially, in the several tales. In *The Bride of Abydos* Selim, leader of a pirate band, loves Giaffir's daughter, Zuleika, who is affianced to an aged man. Because Giaffir, Selim's uncle, has murdered Selim's father, revenge is in order; but Selim refrains out of consideration for Zuleika's feelings. Discovered in rendezvous, Selim is killed, Zuleika dies of heartbreak, and Giaffir is left to avenging solitude.

The *Corsair,* however, departs somewhat from the usual pattern. Conrad, a pirate and rebel against the cruel tyranny of the Seyd Pacha, is captured and condemned to death by impalement. Gulnare, harem favorite of the Seyd, releases Conrad, kills the Seyd; and the two lovers escape to the pirate stronghold where they find that Conrad's mistress, Medora, has died of heartbreak. United by their mutual guilt, Conrad and Gulnare disappear.

In *Lara,* apparently considered by Byron as a sequel to the *Corsair,* Conrad reappears as Lara; Gulnare, as his page Kaled. In a story which has all the trappings of the Gothic tale of terror, Lara is recognized by Ezzelin, who threatens to reveal the former's crimes. Ezzelin is mysteriously murdered; Lara, the suspect, joins the revolting serfs and dies in battle; Kaled, discovered to be a woman, succumbs to madness and death.

In *Parisina,* considered by Calvert the finest of the group, Azo, husband of the beauteous Parisina, discovers that Hugo, his son by a former mistress, is the lover of his wife. He condemns his son to death and his wife to an unrevealed punishment. The strength of the work, in Marshall's judgment, lies in the triangular relationship, both conscious and unconscious, among these persons and especially in the dramatic tension between father and son.[15] Like the earlier Giaffir, who had meted out harsh retribution, Azo does not escape remorse; for "Azo's age was wretched still."

In the last of the group, *The Siege of Corinth,* Byron returns to the Turkish setting and to bizarre Gothicism with a vengeance. In a nightmarish scene, Alp, the renegade from Christian Venice and the indomitable leader of the besieging Moslems, wanders over the battlefield at night where wild dogs rend the bodies of the slain. He is visited by the apparition of his estranged love, Francesca, who pleads with him to renounce the Crescent and to return to the Cross and safety with her. Adamant in his refusal, Alp beholds his love vanish. Next morning, in the storming of the city, Alp encounters Francesca's father, learns of her death the preceding night, and falls victim to a defender's bullet.

I incline to agree with Rutherford that the literary merit of these heroes is slender. Although they obviously surpass the "superficial attitudinising" of *Childe Harold* in concreteness and vitality, their portrayal is achieved by stylistic excesses which reflect at this time "a fundamental immaturity" in Byron. There is no psychological analysis of the protagonists; their superiority to other men lies only in their pride, defiance, intrepidity, and prowess; their dominant motive is revenge; their goal is liberty, anarchic and individualistic, without a trace of moral purpose. In all these portrayals, Byron reveals an element of puerile self-dramatization.[16]

In metrical technique, the Eastern tales are uneven. They range from vigor and competence to carelessness in style and structure; they are marred by occasional lapses in rhyme and rhythm. The original four-hundred-line *Giaour* was balladlike and very effective. The eventual 1334-line version after the addition of accretive stanzas took on a "fragment" character, and it suffered likewise from metrical rigidity imposed by virtually unrelieved octosyllabic couplets. In *The Bride* the poet keeps the octosyllabic base but gives interest by abundant variations of rhyme scheme. In *Corsair* and in *Lara* Byron returns to the heroic couplet and gains episodic unity in the former by the use of the quest theme and in the latter some degree of structural unity by emphasis upon the Ezzelin and Kaled relationship. Byron resumes the octosyllabic couplet in *The Siege of Corinth* except for the Coleridgean variations in the middle which are handled with none of Coleridge's deftness. The octosyllabics in *Parisina,* the last of the group, are not marked by noteworthy metrical distinctions.[17]

IV *Marriage*

Early in February, 1814, Hobhouse returned from his Continental tour; and the two close friends were mutually delighted with their reunion. "He is my best friend," Byron wrote in his journal; and Hobhouse was likewise one of the poet's best critics. Byron respected his judgment in important matters, both literary and personal. Sir Harold Nicolson has rightly called Hobhouse "the balance wheel in Byron's life." Byron, now living in spacious bachelor's quarters in the Albany House in Piccadilly, preferred the intellectual companionship of Hobhouse and congenial literary associations with Samuel Rogers, R. B. Sheridan, and Mme. de Staël to the social whirl of the *haut ton.*

In mid-April the news came that Augusta had given birth to a daughter whom she named Elizabeth Medora. Later, Medora Leigh was to believe herself Byron's daughter, although Byron never acknowledged the paternity, either because he was uncertain or wise enough to keep silent. When, about the same time, Byron received a formal invitation from Annabella's father, Sir Ralph Milbanke, to visit Seaham, Byron's feelings were at war. Bored by the life of high society, alarmed by his obsessive attraction to Augusta, and longing for the sunlit scenes of his Eastern tour, Byron thought of escaping from his entanglements by departure from England or by a sober marriage.

After spending much of the summer with Augusta at the seashore near Hastings and at Newstead, and diplomatically declining the reiterated invitation to Seaham, Byron finally in September wrote to Annabella Milbanke a half-hearted, tentative proposal of marriage. During the ten days until her answer came, Byron was at sixes and sevens: If Annabella accepted — marriage; if not, the Mediterranean with Hobhouse. Annabella, who regarded the proposal as *bona fide,* immediately wrote two letters of acceptance, one to Newstead, the other to London! Lord Byron's fate was sealed.[18]

Byron very strongly hoped and seriously believed that marriage with Annabella Milbanke would help him settle down to a more rational pattern of living and reconcile the conflicts that constantly raged within him. In this good, inexperienced, and serious-minded girl he hoped to find the realization of the ideal he had always sought.[19] In a word, he would try to be what she expected and wanted him to be.

Pressed by his fiancée and her family to come to Seaham, Byron delayed his arrival because of obstacles to the arrangement of his financial affairs and because of reluctance. When he finally left on October 29, he stopped on the way to visit Augusta at Six Mile Bottom and did not arrive at Seaham until November 2. The distraught Annabella hoped that her parents would not notice that Byron had brought no presents and no engagement ring. The conspicuously not ardent lover spent but two uneasy weeks with his betrothed and then returned to London by way of Cambridge and Six Mile Bottom where he again visited Augusta.

Annabella urged Byron to return to Seaham and set a definite date for the wedding. She had hoped that he might at least spend Christmas at Seaham but was grievously disappointed. Byron postponed his departure until December 24, spent Christmas Day with Augusta, and finally arrived at Seaham on December 30 accompanied by Hobhouse, who wrote in his diary, "Never was a lover less in haste."[20] When Byron and Annabella were wedded on January 2, 1815, in the parlor at Seaham in a very sober and inauspicious ceremony, Hobhouse wrote: "I felt as if I had buried a friend."[21]

The cheerless and unromantic forty-mile carriage ride in the winter cold of the newlyweds to Halnaby Hall was followed by a quite unhoneymoonlike three weeks. Byron's alternate moods of tenderness and harshness toward Lady Byron began almost at once. Annabella was distressed by his coolness, irony, and sometimes apparent aversion; but she was exalted when his mood changed to pleasantness and affection. Then he would call his rosy-faced bride "Pippin," and she would respond with "Dear Duck." They read together Scott's Waverley novels, just beginning; and Byron resumed his *Hebrew Melodies,* lyrics for Isaac Nathan's music, which he had begun the previous autumn.

But the sensitive and anxious Annabella had very little inner peace, for her moody husband made unmistakable his deep affection for his sister Augusta and again and again hinted at some dark secret not to be divulged. Significantly, about this time Byron began work on *Parisina* based on a fifteenth-century tragedy of incest. Annabella was wise enough to perceive that beneath Byron's "Satanic" exterior was a fundamental, if unconscious, "gloomy Calvinism" which none of his powers of "reason, wit, and ridicule" would dispel. On the practical side, Annabella was probably not adequately aware that one of the causes of her husband's irascibility throughout their brief marriage was his constant financial harassment. The fifth Lord Byron ("Wicked Lord") had illegally leased in 1784 the coal mines on the Byron family's Rochdale estate in Lancashire for the incredibly small annual rental of sixty pounds. The Rochdale estate litigation, which was to trouble Byron most of his life, continued unresolved and without revenue; and the contemplated sale of Newstead remained unrealized. Lord and Lady Byron were back at Seaham by January 22 and to Moore he wrote, ". . . the treaclemoon is over . . ."[22]

Although Byron gradually became accustomed to domesticity at Seaham, he eventually grew bored and desired to return to London. In March the couple left for London, stopping to visit for several weeks with Augusta at Six Mile Bottom. Lady Byron's days and nights were a torment, but Augusta's were not much easier; for Byron, in his unpredictable black moods baited both women unmercifully but unmistakably revealed his preference for Augusta. Augusta was relieved when the couple departed for No. 13 Piccadilly Terrace in London. Almost inexplicably, Lady Byron invited Augusta to visit them in London, and she did so early in April.

But Byron was more tractable now, occupied with literary interests and congenial associates. He gladly complied with a request from Coleridge for an assist with Murray in securing publication of a volume of poetry. And Byron realized on April 7 his long-standing desire to meet Walter Scott, whom he regarded as the first of living authors; for it was Murray's delight to bring the two popular authors together in his office at 50 Albemarle Street. Their mutual admiration was instant and enduring. Also, in April Byron's *Hebrew Melodies* was published with musical settings by Nathan in a large folio that sold ten thousand copies in two editions. In May Byron became a member of the Sub-Committee of Management of the Drury Lane Theatre on the recommendation of his banker friend, Douglas Kinnaird. Later, when the fall season opened, Byron labored effectively in behalf of the theater, seeking suitable scripts and able dramatic talent. He secured the Irish novelist Charles Robert Maturin's *Bertram* and encouraged Coleridge to attempt a drama for Drury Lane. A further evidence of Byron's openness of mind and critical acumen was his sincere praise of Coleridge's *Christabel* and his apology for his unwarranted animadversions on Coleridge in *English Bards.*

That Byron had not lost interest in political and international affairs is shown by his attendance at Parliament in April to hear the debate on Napoleon's escape from Elba and again in May to vote with the Whigs in their effort to censure the Tory government for its participation in the Congress of Vienna. And, after Napoleon's fall at Waterloo in June, Byron was furious with the Tory government for its acquiescence in the policy of reaction being pursued by the Continental Powers in their efforts to reestablish the old pre-Napoleonic tyrannies in Europe.[23] Later he declared in *Don Juan* his "sworn, downright detestation of every despotism in every nation."

In October Byron completed the latest of his Eastern tales, *The Siege of Corinth.* But literary endeavors were being crowded out by financial harassments. Byron's creditors were hounding him and repeatedly sending bailiffs into his house to make executions. When Murray heard of Byron's agonized decision to sell his library, he made the poet a generous offer for his literary works; but Byron was too proud to accept. Aggravated beyond endurance, Byron was driven into rages that terrified Lady Byron and Augusta. During these fits of irrational behavior, Byron made his wife, now in the advanced stage of pregnancy, the scapegoat for all his troubles. Exaggerated accounts of his behavior at this period have survived; but, apocryphal as some of them may be, his conduct was undeniably harrowing for Lady Byron. Both she and Augusta, who lived in the house during Lady Byron's pregnancy, took refuge in the mistaken thought that Byron might be suffering from temporary insanity.

When Byron's daughter, Augusta Ada, was born on December 10, 1815, he was proud of the child; but her presence failed to reconcile him to his marriage as Lady Byron had hoped. As his money problems grew more acute, his frenzied rages and shocking utterances increased. When, on the first of January, Byron proposed that he and Lady Byron break up their expensive Piccadilly quarters and that she and the child precede him to her parents' home while he completed his efforts to pacify the creditors, she may well have misconceived his motives. Apparently with Augusta's approval, she consulted two medical men, Baillie and Le Mann, regarding her husband's possible temporary insanity, even drawing up a list of his symptoms in support. Later, in *Don Juan* (I, 27-28), in a satirical portrait of his wife as Donna Inez, Byron wrote: "For Inez called some druggists and physicians / And tried to prove her loving lord was mad."

Early in the morning of January 15, 1816, Lady Byron with little Augusta Ada left Picadilly Terrace for Kirkby Mallory in Leicestershire before Byron had risen. The three never met again.

CHAPTER 6

1816 Separation and Exile:
Childe Harold *III*

A T first Lady Byron wrote affectionate letters to Byron in London, urging him to join her at Kirkby Mallory and relaying her parents' best regards and eagerness for his coming. She had told her parents of Byron's affliction, and they shared her hope that country air and exercise might cure him of his temporary mental ailment. However, something — one can only surmise what — prompted her to confide to her parents a realistic account of all she had suffered from Byron during her marriage. From that moment her parents completely altered their attitude toward Byron and they exacted a promise from her never to return to her husband even if he proved to be sane.

Sir Ralph and Lady Noel then set about securing for their daughter legal as well as medical advice with regard to her husband's behavior. Lady Noel went to London to consult Le Mann and Dr. Stephen Lushington, a distinguished barrister; and she also talked with Augusta and Mrs. Clermont, the former governess of Lady Byron and an influential friend who had helped Augusta "protect" Lady Byron from her husband during her pregnancy. Le Mann had found no proofs of Byron's insanity, and Lady Noel was convinced that Byron's conduct was not madness but badness. Dr. Lushington counseled that Lady Byron have nothing more to do with her husband and that Sir Ralph negotiate with Byron for a quiet separation.[1]

I *Separation*

In London, and unaware of all the secret investigations being conducted by Lady Byron's parents, Byron was shocked by the

70

request for a separation. Unable to account for the abrupt change from the congeniality of their last days together and the marked affection of her letters from Kirkby, he refused to accept any change of status unless it was specifically requested by Lady Byron herself; for he suspected Lady Noel and Mrs. Clermont of having influenced his wife against him. When Lady Byron realized that Byron's cruel actions and utterances could not be attributed to derangement, she wrote to assure him that her decision for a separation was self-determined and irrevocable.

The unmistakable sincerity and affection of Byron's reply, clearly opening the door to a reconciliation, was not lost on Annabella, who was torn between her genuine attachment for this most charming and unfathomable of men and her own inflexible sense of duty and strict conscience. In Byron's last appeal to Annabella he wrote: "And now, Bell, dearest Bell ... I can only say in the truth of affliction, and without hope, motive, or end in again saying what I have lately but vainly repeated, that I love you, bad or good, mad or rational, miserable or content, I love you, and shall do, to the dregs of my memory and existence."²

But Lady Byron was adamant; she visited Dr. Lushington in London on February 22 and divulged "facts" that convinced him that the separation from Byron was unavoidable and imperative. What the "facts" were is still a matter of speculation, but it seems clear that Lady Byron confessed her suspicion of incest between Byron and Augusta — and added it to the prior charges of adultery and cruelty.³ Rumors in the London streets that Byron was to be accused of cruelty, drunkenness, and infidelity mingled in mid-February with the news of publication of his two latest Eastern tales, *The Siege of Corinth* and *Parisina*. By the end of February the scandal linking Byron and Mrs. Leigh was everywhere. Hobhouse was so outraged that he drew up a denial of rumored cruelties, incest, and unnamed abominations to be signed by Lady Byron as a condition of separation.⁴ But no amount of denials could stop the rumors.

By March 17 the terms of the legal separation were determined. About this time a young woman quite unknown to Byron began her persistent overtures. At first her letter professing her love and requesting a meeting seemed like only another among the scores of such letters he had received from unknown women during his years of fame. But, as her letters continued, he soon recognized their distinguishing frankness, intelligence, and originality. The girl proved to be Claire Clairmont, the eighteen-year-old, dark-haired, not unattractive stepdaughter of William Godwin and the stepsister of Mary Godwin, with whom Percy Shelley had eloped in 1814. Her association with the "wonder-boy" poet Shelley, whose *Queen Mab* Byron had seen and admired, may have piqued Byron's curiosity and inclined him to tolerate the advances of the importunate Claire. By mid-April the determined girl, who had laid unremitting siege to the famous poet, achieved a casual liaison. But Byron never was in love with her, and he was appalled at the prospect of encountering her again on the Continent, where she planned to go with the Shelleys.[5]

Resigned to his wife's unalterable determination to separate, and planning to depart for the Continent as soon as the separation was formally completed, Byron in mid-March wrote the first of the Poems of the Separation. "Fare thee well! and if forever" addressed to Lady Byron. And shortly after, in a very different mood, he vented his great wrath against Mrs. Clermont, whom he held chiefly responsible for his wife's obduracy, in "A Sketch from Private Life," the bitterest poem he ever wrote.

Byron's dejection deepened when in early April his extensive library was sold at public auction. Further, he was now being snubbed and avoided in the same social circles which had lionized him. Augusta seemed to him "a tower of strength," and her loyal affection was his "last rallying point."[6] In gratitude he composed his first "Stanzas to Augusta," declaring that her loving devotion, "When all around grew drear and dark," was like a "solitary star which rose and set not to the last."[7] Two days later, on April 14, Easter Sunday, Byron and Augusta took their sad farewell of each other, never to meet again.

The next day a London newspaper printed the first two Poems of the Separation, others followed suit; and there ensued a concerted attack on Lord Byron, personal and political, for his alleged mistreatment of his wife. Byron now felt that he was the victim of private contumely and the object of public scorn. However much he may later have exaggerated the general ostracism visited upon him at this time, there can be no question but that Byron genuinely felt himself to be the scapegoat of a hypocritical British society which demanded his exile.

Byron was by now grossly dissatisfied with his "versenovelettes," preferring his earlier heroic couplet satires and the meditative-topographical mode of *Childe Harold.* He realized that he had fully exploited his current medium and needed "fresh woods and pastures new." But he was also well aware that he had not yet found his surest poetic vein. In his continuing search for form, which ultimately led him to *Beppo* and *Don Juan,* Byron was handicapped by what Rutherford tellingly delineates as "his fatal distaste for self-criticism" and by "his persistent insulation of his poetry from his realism and common sense."[8] Something drastic was needed to rescue him from his fictitious role of "Byronic hero" in which society insisted on seeing him and to restore him to himself as a man and poet. The answer to his problem came in the shape of his separation and exile.

II *Exile*

Byron signed the formal deed of separation on April 21. His closest friends, who had never ceased to rally to him, took their reluctant farewells — Hobhouse, Scrope Davies, Kinnaird, Rogers, and Hanson. On the twenty-third he left London for Dover in his huge Napoleonic coach, accompanied by Hobhouse and Davies who were to see him off on the boat. With his servants, William Fletcher and the youth Robert Rushton, Byron waited at Dover for a favorable wind. On the morning of April 25 Byron sailed away, never to return to England. Hobhouse wrote in his diary that day, "...God bless him for a gallant spirit and a kind one..."[9]

Again the roving Childe Harold, but with a difference, Byron only "half realized," as Marchand says, that this was "the end of an epoch in his life, but he was not yet aware to what extent it was the beginning of his maturer literary existence."[10] On the Continent Byron found the opportunity to create for himself a new role as man and poet. Escaping from a superficial and boring social world and from a disillusioning experience of uncongenial domesticity, he was ready to begin the search for his real self and for the poetic form best suited to his genius. The goal was not immediately achieved; the current of his life sometimes eddied and swept him back into moods and expressions of his earlier role; but the essential and ultimate flow was forward; and the quest was undertaken with a deep and genuine sincerity. Increasingly, Byron's interest was drawn to the real world of real people and real experiences, credible, actual, even historical. "From now on," Calvert discerningly writes, "Byron's creative energy, however diverse its form, was bent to a single task — the celebration of unadorned reality."[11]

From Ostend, Byron and his retinue traveled by way of Ghent and Antwerp to Brussels, where he met Major Pryse Lockhart Gordon, who gave him a copy of Giambattista Casti's *Novelle Galanti,* one of the works which later inspired Byron's serio-comic *Beppo* and *Don Juan.* But Byron's mood was deadly serious when, with Gordon, he visited the field of Waterloo:

> And Harold stands upon this place of skulls
> The grave of France, the deadly Waterloo!   5 1-2

From this melancholy experience emerged the famous stanzas on Waterloo in *Childe Harold,* Canto III, and those on Napoleon, whose defeat had not conquered tyranny in Europe. By May 8, Byron was at Cologne, intent upon traveling up the Rhine to Switzerland.

In England, Byron's close friends were doing their best to still the villainous rumors circulating in London. Their efforts were not helped by the publication on May 9 of a novel, *Glenarvon,* by the giddy-headed and vicious Caroline Lamb, in which she represented herself and Byron as the chief characters of the highly exaggerated, excessively romanticized Gothic narrative. And in another quarter of England, Lady Byron, in retirement at Kirkby Mallory, was coolly laying her plans for her campaign against Augusta. Annabella's deliberate, prolonged, and cruel persecution of the lonely, unhappy woman had a twofold purpose: first, to prevail upon Augusta to confess to incest; and, second, to intimidate her into renouncing commerce with or affection for Byron. Lady Byron's jealousy, writes Marchand, "found sublimation in a truly sadistic zeal to extract the sin from Augusta's life and save her." "There are few records of the cruelty that wears a benevolent face, of the studied undermining of the peace of mind of a fellow woman, equal to the deliberate assault upon the conscience of Augusta," he concludes.[12]

III   *With Shelley in Switzerland*

Meanwhile, Byron's travels were providing more stanzas for

Childe Harold as he journeyed up the Rhine valley, past "The castled Crag of Drachenfels," and through the Alps. Reveling in the beauty and grandeur of all he beheld, Byron finally arrived — by way of Basel, the Juras, Morat, and Lausanne — at Geneva on the shores of Lake Leman on May 25. Byron, at Dejean's Hotel d'Angleterre, did not know that Claire Clairmont, with the Shelleys, had preceded him by twelve days. Claire, now carrying Byron's child, had been waiting impatiently for his arrival. But Byron evinced little interest in renewing the liaison.

In contrast, Byron was very pleased to meet Shelley, the youthful author of *Queen Mab*. This meeting was the beginning of the genuine friendship and mutual high regard that persisted between the two poets. Their joint house-hunting efforts were soon rewarded. By the beginning of June Byron had taken the Villa Diodati situated on a hill near Cologny on the south shore of the lake commanding a splendid panoramic view of Lake Leman and the Jura Mountains. The Shelleys, with Claire Clairmont, were delighted with their small house at Montalègre at the foot of the hill. The two poets bought a small sailing boat which they kept in the small private harbor near Shelley's house. Byron found the Shelley menage altogether agreeable — both Shelley and Mary were unconventional, intellectual, and imaginative companions; and Claire adequately satisfied his physical desires in the casual relationship which he half-heartedly resumed with the importunate young woman. When the weather permitted, Byron and Shelley sailed by day on Lake Leman and took the young women with them for moonlight cruises. In stormy weather, they sat around the fire in Byron's villa engaged in conversation or in the telling and writing of ghost stories. Each began one, but only Mary took it seriously and wrote *Frankenstein*.

All these experiences of mountain, lake and sky, and the stimulating conversation with Shelley were providing Byron with material for more stanzas of *Childe Harold*. Especially is Shelley's influence apparent in the Wordsworthian pantheistic mood of certain stanzas of the third canto of *Childe Harold:*

> I live not in myself, but I become   7
> Portion of that around me; and to me
> High mountains are a feeling...

But this mood was a passing one with Byron and not typical of his view of nature.[13]

IV   The Prisoner of Chillon

In June, the two poets made a tour of Lake Leman in their sailboat. At one point, when their small craft was threatened by a severe storm, Byron, a powerful swimmer, assured Shelley that he could save him if the boat capsized; but Shelley, though he was unable to swim, remained unperturbed throughout. They visited the picturesque fortified Chateau de Chillon where Byron was inspired by the story of François Bonivard, sixteenth-century patriot and political prisoner, to conceive his famous poem *The Prisoner of Chillon,* in which he tells for the first time a dramatic tale of a real person, in the actual world, and based on a foundation of historical fact.

Unquestionably the best of Byron's verse tales, the poem exemplifies the poet's increasing tendency toward "the celebration of unadorned reality." The "Sonnet on Chillon," which precedes the verse tale of Bonivard, celebrates the invincible spirit of liberty: "Eternal Spirit of the chainless Mind!/Brightest in dungeons, Liberty! thou art..." Bonivard, chained to his dungeon pillar, is truly, as Marchand says, a "Promethean figure" who became for Byron and has remained for innumerable readers the embodiment of the "chainless mind" that "defies intolerance and tyranny and of the defiant courage of a man willing to suffer for a principle."[14]

With a moral purpose thus clearly conceived, Byron proceeds with admirable swiftness, clarity, and concreteness to the delineation of his narrator-protagonist, his background, and the circumstances and the place of his imprisonment:

> My hair is grey, but not with years,
> Nor grew it white in a single night,
> As men's have grown from sudden fears:
> My limbs are bowed, though not with toil,
> But rusted with a vile repose,
> For they have been a dungeon's spoil,
>
> . . . .
> But this was for my father's faith
> I suffered chains and courted death...   6

With swift and vigorous strokes, the poet describes the dungeon,
the columns, the prison chains, and fetters:

> There are seven pillars of Gothic mold,
> In Chillon's dungeons deep and old,
> There are seven columns, massy and grey,
> Dull with a dim imprisoned ray,
> . . . .
> And in each pillar there is a ring,
> And in each ring there is a chain;
> That iron is a cankering thing,
> For in these limbs its teeth remain. . .

Lucidly, and with scrupulous attention to realistic details, the poet
depicts the setting of the chateau and its dungeon hall beneath the
surface of the lake; and he sharply contrasts the liberty of Nature
with human incarceration, an antithesis which Rutherford calls the
poem's "fundamental contrast between Freedom and Imprisonment . . . between Life and Death"[15]:

> Lake Leman lies by Chillon's walls:
> A thousand feet in depth below
> Its massy waters meet and flow;
> . . . .
> A double dungeon wall and wave
> Have made—and like a living grave.
> Below the surface of the lake
> The dark vault lies wherein we lay:
> We heard it ripple night and day;

The narrator-protagonist and his two brothers endure his death-
in-life existence until his kinsmen droop and die, leaving him alone:
"I had no thought, no feeling — none — / Among the stones I
stood a stone. . ." In this trancelike condition of insensibility the
speaker remains, broken only by a brief, perhaps symbolic, visit
from a bird at the barred window slit, until his keepers free him
from his column to walk about his dungeon.

When, after the lapse of months or years, unexpected release at
last comes to the prisoner, the reader has been so effectively condi-
tioned by the poem's realism that he almost shares the narrator-
protagonist's apathy and bewilderment:

It was at length the same to me,
Fettered or fetterless to be,

. . . .

My very chains and I grew friends,
So much a long communion tends
To make us what we are: — even I
Regained my freedom with a sigh.

A dramatic monologue in form and in octosyllabic couplets, with some variation in rhyme scheme, the *Prisoner of Chillon* represents the achievement of an artistic-moral purpose with an economy and force that are new in Byron's writings.[16] The poem is superior to any of Byron's work that preceded it, not only in technique but in deeper human understanding, sounder values, and greater integrity of feeling. The narrator-protagonist is also more credible, consistent, and mature than prior hero-protagonists; and he is free from the faults of the familiar "Byronic hero." "*The Prisoner of Chillon* is a more finished, satisfying work of art," writes Rutherford, "than any of Byron's poems up to this date."[17]

V   Childe Harold *III*

By July 1 the two poet-sailors were back at Cologny. Three days later Byron finished the third canto of *Childe Harold*. The work is not a "premeditated work of art" but an impulsive reaction in verse to his recent ordeal of separation and exile and a poetic expression of the feelings and reflections engendered by his new travel experiences. The poet returns to the eighteenth-century mode of topographical-meditative poetry, employed in his earlier *Childe Harold;* but he brings to it the new virtues of scrupulosity of treatment, authenticity of material, and virtuosity of technique.

Admitting his failure to establish and maintain a distinction between himself and his titular hero, the poet frankly abandons the effort: "The fact is, that I had become weary of drawing a line which everyone seemed determined not to perceive . . . . I determined to abandon it altogether — and have done so."[18] Henceforth, the poet speaks in his own right and, with minor exceptions, obliterates the prior distinction between hero and narrator. Harold becomes a shadowy wraith in the background who eventually, in the last canto, vanishes altogether.

In fact, the central feature of *Childe Harold,* Canto III, Rutherford asserts, is this fusion of the poet with his hero. The new protagonist, combining the functions of hero and narrator, still
expresses most of the familiar qualities of the earlier Harold —
melancholy, solitariness, and passion — but, at the same time and
more importantly, he voices Byron's personal sufferings, his rebellious pride, and his indignant outrage over the ostracism accorded
him by a hypocritical society. Unlike the earlier Harold, the new
protagonist is no longer an *ennui*-ridden Gloomy Wanderer or outlaw Hero but the figure of the Poet — "the wronged and suffering
Romantic Genius."[19]

Contemporary critics differ somewhat regarding the chief theme,
or themes, of Canto III. For Marshall, it is isolation. The apostrophe to the poet's daughter — the dramatic framing device —
opens and closes the canto. Within this framework the theme of
isolation is represented in a series of projected elements — the
battlefield of Waterloo, Napoleon, the focal Rhine journey, Rousseau, and the Alps — which provide organic cohesion.[20] Calvert
finds Canto III "metaphysical"; its theme is "the sympathetic
investigation of madness, or of those souls who make men mad by
their contagion — Napoleon and Rousseau..."[21] In Rutherford's
comprehensive view there are four chief foci of interest which, seen
through the eye of the narrator-hero and assimilated to the poet-
hero's personality and preoccupations, give rise to passages of
lively and personal introspection and reflection. These four major
themes — the poet's "wrongs and sorrows, the fate of genius [such
as Napoleon and Rousseau], the liberty of peoples, the value and
significance of Nature" — are interwoven and related to the poet-
hero's mind and character, imposing a satisfying coherence on
what would otherwise be a welter of observations and reflections.[22]

Within the framing device of the poet's apostrophe to his little
daughter, Ada, the first of the four chief foci of interest is the poet-
hero's preoccupation with his own wrongs and sorrows: "In my
youth's summer I did sing of One, / The wandering outlaw of his
own dark mind. . . ." And, irritatingly, he hints at "deeds without
a name" which have aged him beyond his years: "He, who grown
agéd in this world of woe, / In deeds, not years, piercing the depths
of life, / So that no wonder waits him..." And the romantic
notion of alienation from society and preferred solitariness suits
with the poet's mood of rebellious pride: "But soon he knew him-

self the most unfit / Of men to herd with Man, with whom he held / Little in common..."

But, fortunately, these reprehensibly self-pitying and complacent moods do not continue as Byron moves on to the next focus of interest, the fate of genius to be misunderstood and depreciated by inferior men. In passages of unexpectedly sound and objective analysis of the psychology of Napoleon and Rousseau, Byron delineates the faults as well as virtues of these two geniuses "who have made men mad by their contagion." This section contains what Calvert calls Byron's "sympathetic investigation of madness."[23]

> But Quiet to quick bosoms is a Hell,
> And *there* hath been thy bane; ...
> . . . .
> This makes the madmen who have made men mad
> By their contagion; Conquerors and Kings,
> Founders of sects and systems, to whom add
> Sophists, Bards, Statesmen, all unquiet things
> Which stir too strongly the soul's secret springs,   3 1-2
> And are themselves the fools to those they fool; ...

And Byron distinguishes Rousseau's greatnesses and his fatal delusions:

> Here the self-torturing sophist, wild Rousseau,
> The apostle of affliction, he who threw
> Enchantment over Passion, and from Woe
> Wrung overwhelming eloquence, ...
> . . . .
> For then he was inspired, and from him came,
> As from the Pythian's mystic cave of yore,
> Those oracles which set the world in flame,   4 1-2
> Nor, ceased to burn till kingdoms were no more.

Some of Byron's most eloquent rhetoric is reserved for the third chief theme, the liberty of peoples, as the poet-hero visits the battle-fields of Waterloo and Morat. Byron reveals some of his most deeply felt and lasting views on wars and politics. His hatred of despotism, which later in *Don Juan* he declared as his "sworn, downright detestation of every despotism in every nation," and his quick concern for the oppressed, whether from domestic or foreign tyrants, appear in these stanzas. The same motives that prompted him as a Harrow boy to champion the underdog, as a youthful Parliamentarian to defend the frame-breakers of Nottingham, and as a man to lay down his life for the liberation of Greece, are here operative. He despised wars of aggression and conquest as ruthless, indefensible, and futile; he justified only the wars for liberation of peoples, such as that waged by the ancient Greeks at Marathon or by the colonists in the American Revolution. And there follows the famous declamatory favorite of our fathers which, though it may represent a sinking in matter and style from the preceding and following high seriousness, is yet emotionally moving: "There was a sound of revelry by night..."

But Byron now turns to celebrate the Battle of Morat, fought justifiably for liberty by the Swiss against the Burgundians: "While Waterloo with Cannae's carnage vies, / Morat and Marathon twin names shall stand; / They were true Glory's stainless victories..."

Fourth, and last, of the chief themes of Canto III is the value and significance of Nature. Under the immediate influence of the Alps, Lake Leman, and Wordsworth's nature pantheism — ministered to him by Shelley — Byron temporarily expresses a kind of reflected Nature mysticism. In Joseph's phrase, this is Byron's "summer mood" — a "sense of romantic expansiveness and communion inspired by the scenery of the Alps and Lac Leman."[24]

> I live not in myself, but I become
> Portion of that around me; and to me
> High mountains are a feeling,...
> . . . .
> And thus I am absorbed, and this is life: —   4 1-2
> Are not the mountains, waves, and skies, a part
> Of me and of my Soul, as I of them?
> Is not the love of these deep in my heart
> With a pure passion?...

Joseph is right in his view that this is not a spurious sentiment on Byron's part but an extreme example of his *"mobilité"* — a "surrender to these persuasive influences of the moment" which gave him a "momentary sense of peace and exaltation."[25] But it was a passing mood because it was foreign to Byron's essential view of

Nature — one in which Nature symbolizes for him his own personality and emotions writ large.[26] As soon as Byron leaves Shelley
and the "Rousseau-haunted" Lake Leman, his habitual realism
returns. On a tour of the Bernese Alps in September, 1816, with
Hobhouse, all the terrible grandeur and glory of glaciers, storms,
avalanches, and torrents, and the majesty of the Jungfrau itself,
could not for one moment, Byron wrote, "lighten the weight upon
my heart, nor enable me to lose my own wretched identity."[27] He
can neither escape from himself in nature nor find Wordsworthian
"healing power"; instead, he finds his own conflicts and sufferings
magnified almost intolerably.

Robert F. Gleckner, in his *Byron and The Ruins of Paradise,*
focuses on Byron's poems through 1816 and depicts him as a modern poet-prophet of doom who had a consistent dark vision of the
human condition after the Fall. Byron's "prophetic view of the
past and of his own time," Gleckner observes, "develops gradually
into the myth of man's external fall and damnation into the hell of
human existence, the myth of what I choose to call the ruins of
paradise and the consequent human condition."[28] As for Byron's
voice, it "is that of man eternally alive and feeling amidst a universe of death that is eternally bent on perpetuating chaos and
nothingness."[29] "If in his poetry," Gleckner concludes, "there is
little evidence of a Romantic construct, a world ever created anew,
a system of belief however personal, his voice crying out in accents
of the human heart will be, if not so oracular as Shelley's, still a
'contagion to the world.' For it is upon his ruins of paradise that all
future building must take place."[30]

Byron's inability to comprehend, much less to accept, benevolent
naturalism as essentially foreign to his way of thought and feeling
is, in fact, a blessing in disguise. To lose his "own wretched identity" and to discover a genuine form of self-liberation he had, as
Joseph discerns, "to rediscover the other form of liberation
through art, and to perfect the Juanesque form which would allow
him literally to stand aside from himself, and to be simultaneously
involved and detached."[31] His summer experience in Switzerland in
1816 was a step, therefore, in the right direction.

Clearly, Canto III is more prepossessing than the earlier cantos.
The poet handles his material with more force and skill and, not
infrequently, he achieves stylistic elevation. To W. Paul Elledge in
his *Byron and the Dynamics of Metaphor,* Byron's most frequent

and representative images reflect the essential dichotomy of human nature and dramatize the pathos and tragedy of mortality. "Given the elastic and exploratory qualities of Byron's thought," Elledge writes, "one might expect the most frequent and representative images in his poetry to bear upon the dichotomies in man's character."[32] "Byron's images . . . function actively as complements and reinforcements to his themes; thus they represent . . . the ultimate union of his intellectual and imaginative faculties."[33] A close study of representative poetry indicates, Elledge concludes, "that Byron recognized the value of employing imagery for thematic purposes and that he attempted to refine, to sharpen his images, to give them depth and force by accretion and particularity, and to integrate them organically with his themes."[34]

Unfortunately there is sinking, when the matter fails to sustain the high style; and there are also recurring imprecisions in diction and imagery. But these are primarily faults of careless craftsmanship. More serious is what Rutherford deplores as the poet's "self-flattering, self-dramatising self deception . . . which appears again and again, producing some of the most famous, but most questionable, purple passages in Canto III . . . . Here we have the Byronic Byron at his best and worst."[35] Apropos of this Byronic Byron, Gilbert Phelps has recently spoken strongly for his "best": "The recent tendency to split Byron into two very unequal parts," with almost exclusive emphasis on *Don Juan,* "has resulted in a lack of balance that fails to do justice to the poetry of the Byronic Byron."[36] Phelps declares that, "if *Don Juan* represents the crown of Byron's poetic achievement, it is certainly time that the Byronic Byron had his day."[37]

But more fundamental in Canto III is an uncertainty in the conception of the character of the titular hero. Here Byron is trying for the first time to combine "romantic liberalism" — revolutionary indoctrination and the liberty of peoples — with the familiar Byronic Hero qualities of misanthropy, solitariness, and pride. But, when the effort does not succeed, we are confronted with an unresolved contradiction in Byron's own thoughts and feelings.[38] In sum, the limitations of the hero-protagonist mode of presentation in *Childe Harold,* Canto III, are conspicuous. Byron has not yet achieved the masterful separation of hero and narrator which he reaches in *Don Juan.*

VI   *"Home-Thoughts, From Abroad"*

While the Shelley party was away on a visit to Chamouni and
Mont Blanc, Byron's thoughts returned to his last painful experiences in England. At this time he wrote "The Dream," with its
sad account of his failure to realize the ideal love originally inspired
by Mary Chaworth; "Darkness," like a prophecy of a manless
world after a world cataclysm; and "Prometheus," celebrating his
favorite defiant hero from his boyhood. But especially, in his
aloneness at Diodati, Byron's thoughts turned again with love and
appreciation to the one nearest and dearest who had never deserted
him in his extremity; and he wrote more "Stanzas to Augusta"
beginning "Though the day of my Destiny's over." Little did he
realize the deliberate persecution his sister was undergoing at the
hands of Lady Byron. Later in the summer Byron wrote an "Epis-
tle to Augusta" in which he hinted at the intimacy of their relationship, acknowledged with manly frankness his exclusive responsibility for becoming "The careful pilot of my proper woe," and
expressed remorse for the suffering he had brought to Augusta.

With the Shelleys about to return to England and with Byron
expecting to leave soon for Italy, plans had to be made for the care
of the child of Claire and Byron. The Shelleys were willing to have
Claire live with them in England, and Byron agreed to support and
educate the child when it was born; but he refused to have any further relationship whatsoever with Claire. On August 29 the Shelleys
and Claire departed, taking with them *Childe Harold,* Canto III;
The Prisoner of Chillon; and Byron's other shorter poems of the
summer. Claire never saw or heard directly from Byron again.

Fortunately for Byron, two of his best friends from England
arrived just as the Shelleys were leaving. With Hobhouse and
Scrope Davies, Byron visited the Vale of Chamouni and magnificent Mont Blanc. In mid-September, after Davies had left, Byron
and Hobhouse made a twelve-day tour of the Bernese Alps. Both
men were deeply impressed by the majesty of the mountains, and
Byron found the grandeur of the Jungfrau beyond description —
the glaciers, storms, avalanches, torrents. Near the Wengen Alp
and the Wetterhorn, Byron saw a withered forest that reminded
him of himself and his family.[39] Returning by way of Bern and
Fribourg, Byron wrote in his journal that all the majesty of the

Alps he had witnessed could not make him forget his recent "home desolation" or lose his "own wretched identity."[40]

VII Manfred

Back at Villa Diodati, Byron found a letter from Shelley, who rightly discerned the potential poetic greatness of Byron and who challenged him to "some greater enterprise of thought..."[41] Byron welcomed the idea, but felt that he must first purge his mind and spirit: all his suffering, guilt, and remorse he would pour into a new work conceived in the Alps. As the vehicle for his catharsis he chose a form new to him, poetic drama. His intention was not drama for the theater, but a closet drama, or rather, in his own words, "not a drama properly ... but a dialogue."[42] Initially suggested, perhaps by "Monk" Lewis' translation of *Faust,* the work was to have more of a Promethean than a Faustian quality. The real drama was in Byron's mind, a fusion of the cosmic with the personal conflict.[43] Manfred, the protagonist, is essentially Byron. And, though the poetic form is a departure for the poet, the matter is familiar — Byron's personal problems and feelings.

Byron reverts to the Byronic Hero type for his protagonist and gives him the maximum treatment in *Manfred.* As Professor Samuel C. Chew remarks, "Manfred is the consummation of the Byronic hero-type. . . .A depth of thought is given to the melancholy which in the poems of his youth had been merely fashionable."[44] The literary sources of *Manfred,* though Byron was largely unconscious of them, are numerous and eclectic. Among the parallels noted by Chew are Goethe's *Faust,* brought to Byron's notice by "Monk" Lewis' verbal translation at Diodati in the summer of 1816; *Werther;* Chateaubriand's *René;* the Gothic novel and drama generally and in particular Walpole's *Castle of Otranto* and *The Mysterious Mother,* Maturin's *Bertram,* Coleridge's *Remorse,* Shelley's *Queen Mab* and *Alastor,* and "Monk" Lewis' *Vathek.*[45]

But, as Joseph reminds us, Byron declared his chief literary debt to be the *Prometheus* of Aeschylus. Prometheus, who had long been Byron's favorite defiant hero, was much in his mind during the summer of 1816. In fact, in July he had written a short poem, "Prometheus," celebrating the Titan's heroic courage, endurance of suffering, and defiant integrity. But, whereas Aeschylus' Prometheus defies the gods, Manfred defies the powers of evil; and he is therefore closer to the tradition of Faust and to the hero of Shelley's *Prometheus Unbound*.[46]

Begun in Switzerland shortly after the poet's Alpine tour with Hobhouse, *Manfred* reflects Byron's new attitude toward Nature, his rejection of Wordsworthian benevolism and his awareness of the inefficacy of Nature to free *himself* from *himself* and enable him to lose his "own wretched identity." Closely associated is Byron's sense of the destructive powers of evil, related in his mind to Georges Cuvier's concept of recurring cosmic catastrophism. This last concept is the theme of the apocalyptic poem "Darkness" — composed about the same time as "Prometheus" — but even more remarkable in its sinister appropriateness to a manless world following world cataclysm.

Byron wrote the first two acts of *Manfred* in Switzerland and the third in Venice. In its original form the work was cluttered, shapeless, and ineffective; and no one realized this chaos more than Byron who disparaged his "drama" as a "Bedlam tragedy" and "too metaphysical." "The third act is certainly damned bad."[47] When he learned that Gifford concurred with his opinion of the last act, Byron replaced it with a greatly improved version, written under the inspiration of his visit to Rome. The revised Act III saved and transformed the work, giving it whatever significance it possesses.

Manfred has long evoked, and continues to elicit, differing interpretations of its principal theme. Marshall regards the work as a "morality play" that is not concerned with the relation between good and evil but is "essentially concerned with the consciousness or the Self" and is, "broadly, a psychological rather than a philosophic drama."[48] To Calvert, "Manfred is the projection of a mood on a screen . . . the poetical threshing out of a vital personal problem. . ."[49] Rutherford concurs with E. H. Coleridge's observation that "The *motif* of *Manfred* is remorse — eternal suffering for inexpiable crime,"[50] and he regards the play as "a progressive revelation of the hero's character and history . . . in his search for an escape from guilt."[51]

At the beginning of the play, Manfred, self-accused and remorse-ridden over a nameless crime, invokes the Spirits of Nature and the Star of his own destiny, all of which are overruled by a Spirit of recurring cataclysmic destruction. Manfred demands of the Spirits "forgetfulness," though of what guilty secret we are not told. They cannot grant his request, for their power is only over the external elements, not the internal self. A Spirit now takes the form of a beautiful woman, perhaps Astarte, his lost love, and pronounces the curse of selfhood: "I call upon thee! and compel / Thyself to be thy proper Hell!"

Alone on the Jungfrau in Scene II, Manfred contemplates the beauties of Nature, realizes their inefficacy to bring him cure, is horrified by the thought of Nature's destructive power, and attempts suicide, only to be saved by the Chamois Hunter. The ensuing dialogue in Act II between Manfred and the Hunter affords the poet opportunity for one of his favorite themes — the superiority of the aristocratic, sinful, suffering superman-hero over ordinary mortals.

In Scene II Manfred conjures up the Witch of the Alps and relates the tragic story of his love for Astarte and her death, hinting at incest and his consequent remorse and desire for forgetfulness. In Scene IV Astarte appears, and Manfred recognizes her as the spirit of the "One" who understands him, the "One" whom he loved, but destroyed, "Not with my hand, but heart, which broke her heart...."

> Astarte! my beloved! speak to me....
> Thou lovedst me
> Too much, as I loved thee: we were not made
> To torture thus each other — though it were
> The deadliest sin to love as we have loved.

Joseph's observation regarding Manfred's remorse is persuasive. Manfred's guilt may be peculiar to him, but "his predicament is general .... Manfred's real guilt is that he is a member of the human race."[52]

Manfred dares in the last scene of Act II to accost the power of evil itself, the devil Arimanes, personification of the destructive power of Nature. He defies Arimanes, knowing there is a higher power than his, good though inscrutable. Nemesis calls up for Manfred the Phantom of Astarte, who speaks only to inform him of his imminent death, a consummation he has desired.

The original third act worked out no adequate solution to the problem of Manfred's guilt and remorse. The Abbot, a religious zealot and hypocrite, threatened Manfred and met with undignified

retaliation. In a last scene Manfred met with a contrived and melodramatic death. In the revised version, the Abbot is a genuine
Christian who witnesses Manfred's repulsion of the fiends who
come to claim him and remains with Manfred to his dignified
death.

Critical assessment of the significance and value of *Manfred* in
relation to Byron's total poetic achievement is varied. Rutherford
finds "touches of real spiritual dignity in *Manfred*," but he hastens
to point out the serious defects in the character of Manfred which
disqualify him as "in any sense a representative or champion of
Mankind."[53] Lacking a consistent "intellectual substructure,
Manfred soon becomes repetitive, obscure, and muddled. . . ."[54]

Joseph grants that the style of *Manfred* is uneven: some of the
soliloquies are powerful and eloquent, but the choral passages frequently sink to a jingle. It is often ambiguous, but it is better than
"repetitive, obscure, and muddled." Its ambiguities are due to "a
confusion of genres" — the poet's attempt to make the Gothic conventions carry a "weight of introspection or analysis" which they
cannot sustain. This error Byron himself soon realized when he
came to regard both his *Childe Harold* III and *Manfred* as "too
metaphysical" and rejected the Gothic forms in favor of the Classical Unities in his forthcoming dramas. The basic positions of *Manfred*, Joseph maintains, "are consistent with those of his maturity:
belief in a Creator, a doubtful assent to immortality, an increasingly respectful rejection of established religion, and a strong sense
of recurrent violence in the universe. Manfred's defiance, however
confused its origins, is in the end rational, and his death achieves a
stoic pride."[55]

In summary, "Manfred was at bottom Byron," as Calvert
declares. The problem proposed in the first two acts of the play is
essentially Byron's personal problem. The solution finally comes to
him "suggested by an old faint memory from Milton. . . .It creates
a new third act, and it voices to him a reason for living. . . . his art is
no longer the expression of idle moments or unsatisfied desires.
There is no more question of the conscience of art apart from the
conscience of the man."[56] "My pang shall find a voice"[57] is Byron
speaking through Manfred. Having achieved catharsis of his suffering, guilt, and remorse, Byron is ready to move another step
toward the realistic self-knowledge and emancipation of *Don Juan*.

CHAPTER 7

1816–1817 Byron in Italy: Childe Harold *IV*

O N October 5, 1816, Byron, with Hobhouse, took a reluctant farewell of Lake Leman and set out for the journey through the Simplon Pass to Milan and Venice. Passing along the shores of Lago Maggiore, they crossed the Lombardy plain in Byron's Napoleonic coach and reached Milan where Byron was charmed with the cathedral, La Scala, and Italian society. Ludivico Di Breme introduced him to Italian literary men and to the French author Henri Beyle (Stendhal). Byron was especially delighted with the gay political and social satires of Pietro Buratti in the Venetian dialect. On the serious side, Byron learned of the discontent of the Lombardians and Piedmontese with the Austrian overlordship following the Congress of Vienna (1815). When his dislike for Austrian tyranny became known, Byron's movements were thenceforth carefully watched by the Austrian secret police and his association with Italian intransigents observed.[1]

Byron and Hobhouse set out for Venice on November 2 by way of Verona and Padua. Byron was delighted with the magical city of canals, gondolas, palaces, and towers, floating on the waves: "She looks a sea Cybele, fresh from Ocean, / Rising with her tiara of proud towers..." Visiting the Doges Palace, Byron was moved by the story of Marino Faliero, whose tragedy he later dramatized: "I stood in Venice on the 'Bridge of Sighs'; / A Palace and a prison on each hand...."

Taking rooms over a draper's shop near the Piazza San Marco, Byron soon was in love with the draper's dark-eyed wife, Marianna Segati. With this beautiful young woman he established a liaison according to the proper Italian conventions by which a wife might have a lover accepted in society as the *amico* or "friend" not only of the wife but also of the husband. Invited to attend the *conversazione* of the Countess Albrizzi, he met leaders of the literary and social life of Venice, including Ugo Foscolo and the noted sculptor Antonio Canova.

Back home in England, Murray published *Childe Harold,* Canto III, on November 18 and *The Prisoner of Chillon and Other Poems* on December 5. Within a week Murray had sold seven thousand of each. With the additional adventures of Harold, Byron had recaptured his British audience.[2] Byron was sobered by the gloomy news from Shelley of the increasing discontent of the British under the repressive measures of the Tory government and Parliament; but the news imparted casually by the Shelleys that Claire Clairmont had given birth to a daughter January 12 was indifferently received by Byron.

In February Byron joined gaily in the uninhibited revelry of the pre-Lenten Carnival but not to the neglect of all literary endeavor. Sometime during the fever of the Carnival he finished *Manfred,* and he also wrote at this time, "So We'll Go No More A-Roving," perhaps his most beautiful lyric:

> So we'll go no more a-roving
>   So late into the night,
> Though the heart be still as loving,
>   And the moon be still as bright.
>
> For the sword outwears its sheath,
>   And the soul wears out the breast,
> And the heart must pause to breathe,
>   And love itself have rest.
>
> Though the night was made for loving,
>   And the day returns too soon,
> Yet we'll go no more a-roving
>   By the light of the moon.

Debilitated by the prolonged revelry and dissipations of the Carnival, the old sense of aimlessness and dissatisfaction returned; and he wished for some commitment of his life beyond literature, one perhaps political or military. He was eager to join Hobhouse in Rome, but he was too ill with a protracted fever to leave Venice before April. Encouraged by word from Murray of Gifford's enthusiasm for *Manfred,* Byron left in mid-April by way of Ferrara and Florence for Rome. Awed by the ancient grandeur of the Eternal City, he first finished his revision of the third act of *Manfred;* then, with Hobhouse, he absorbed the majestic sights of Rome and transmuted them into new stanzas for a fourth canto of *Childe Harold.*

Back in Venice by the end of May, Byron took the Villa Foscarini at La Mira on the Brenta River seven miles from Venice. There he could escape from the summer heat of Venice; engage in one of his favorite pleasures, horseback riding; and enjoy frequent visits from Marianna Segati; indeed, Byron at La Mira was in one of his happiest periods. During the summer he worked, *con amore,* on a fourth canto of *Childe Harold* in which he first paid tribute to Venice, "the greenest isle" of his imagination, and then celebrated all the sublimities of Rome, at the same time expressing his deepest personal thoughts and feelings. The only flaw in his otherwise idyllic summer was Byron's anxiety about English reaction to his *Manfred.* His apprehension was justified when, after its quiet publication on June 16, it was severely attacked in a London paper for its treatment of incest.[3] However, Byron did not allow this experience to diminish the creative zeal with which he pursued the writing of the fourth, and unquestionably the best, canto of *Childe Harold.*

I   Childe Harold *IV*

Childe Harold IV, begun in Venice in July, 1817, after Byron's inspiring visit to Rome, is essentially a separate and distinct poem from the earlier cantos. After spending the winter of 1816 in Venice, Byron had visited Rome for several weeks in April and May, 1817, absorbing with Hobhouse the majestic sights of the Eternal City. Back in Venice, Byron composed rapidly, finishing the original shape of Canto IV by mid-July; but he continued to revise and add accretive stanzas to the initial matrix until the end of the year.[4]

Enjoying once more the close association with his common-sense friend, Hobhouse, who was at work on his *Historical Notes* for Canto IV, Byron's essential realism reasserted itself; he returned to the congenial historical and antiquarian interests of Canto III and to his sense of time and change. In the section on the ruins of

Rome, the poet goes back to the Renaissance tradition of Petrarch and Poggio; and the spirit of Gibbon's final chapter — the triumph of time over all things mortal — permeates the fourth canto.[5]

The framework of Canto IV is a travel pattern comparable with that of Canto III in which the route was Belgium, the Rhine, and Switzerland. Only now the journey is from Venice to Rome. We are much indebted to Joseph for an excellent outline of the structure of Canto IV with its original matrix and numerous revisions and accretions, as well as for a detailed analysis of the canto.[6] Joseph convincingly demonstrates that Canto IV, the longest section of *Childe Harold's Pilgrimage,* is in its original shape firm and symmetrical. It constitutes "a kind of debate between art and Nature" in two almost equal parts: the first, concerned with Venice and the journey to Rome; the second, with Rome itself; and the two completed with a coda, Byron's famous apostrophe to the ocean.

The narrator-hero device developed in Canto III for the presentation of the poet's surroundings and experiences is ostensibly the same in Canto IV but, neglected, dwindles away. The poet is now speaking in his own right, even as he had declared in the Preface, "With regard to the conduct of the last canto, there will be found less of the pilgrim than in any of the preceding, and that little slightly, if at all, separated from the author speaking in his own person."[7] In his continuing quest for the most appropriate and effective mode of poetic self-expression, Byron is slowly making progress.

Neither is Canto IV only a panorama of Byron's Italian experience and journey to Rome; for, as Marchand correctly observes, it is "also, as usual, a history of his deepest feelings and his inner conflicts during its creation."[8] A certain degree of the melancholy and pessimism of the earlier cantos lingers, and reappears, although it is not the dominant mood of Canto IV. However, Gleckner epitomizes the canto as "an extraordinary imaginative journey into nothingness and despair. . . ."[9] More pervasive is the elegiac mood evoked by the "ruins-of-time" — past civilizations, cities, and relics. And the more manly tone of Byron's recognition of the transcendence of human nobility and genius over change, decay, and death is a welcome innovation. Viewing his own wrongs and rejection in the light of this perspective, he finds comfort and takes heart.

Byron's changed attitude toward Nature forms the background

of his elegiac meditations on the "ruins-of-time." No longer seeking in Nature solace and mystical absorption, he has learned to prize Nature for its sheer beauty and its human associations — historical, literary, artistic, and architectural. The Canto opens with the celebration of Venice, floating on the Adriatic waters like "a sea Cybele, fresh from Ocean," redolent of historical and literary associations:

> I stood in Venice, on the "Bridge of Sighs;"
> A Palace and a prison on each hand:
> I saw from out the wave her structures rise   3
> As from the stroke of the Enchanter's wand:
> A thousand Years their cloudy wings expand
> Around me, and a dying Glory smiles
> O'er the far times, when many a subject land
> Look to the winged Lion's marble piles,
> Where Venice sate in state, throned on her hundred isles!

The immortal figures of Shylock and Othello and Otway's Pierre repeople the Rialto and "cannot be swept or worn away" even though the "keystones of the Arch" should fall.

Later, on the southern journey and in Rome, the poet celebrates "the transcendence of human limitations by art" in the form of such great sculptures as the Venus de Medici, the Laocoön, and the Apollo Belvedere — "the divine embodied in human form and immortalized in marble."[10] And not only literature and sculpture but especially architecture demonstrates this transcendence. Description of and reflection on the ruins of Rome occupies much of Canto IV. The Rome of Byron's day was a landscape overgrown and almost reclaimed by Nature — before the heyday of archaeology — and thus a reconciliation, of sorts, was achieved between art and Nature. But a more perfect harmony between the two results when the grandeur of man's constructions rivals the sublimity of Nature, as in the Colosseum by moonlight:

> Oh, Rome! my Country! City of the Soul!
> The orphans of the heart must turn to thee,
> Lone Mother of dead Empires!...
> . . . .
> The Niobe of nations! there she stands,
> Childless and crownless, in her voiceless woe;

> An empty urn within her withered hands,
> Whose holy dust was scattered long ago;. . .

Other thoughts arise in Byron's mind which are a continuation and development of his concern in the earlier cantos with tyranny and freedom in the Napoleonic and post-Napoleonic eras. Canto IV reflects Byron's ever-increasing concern with the liberation and freedom of peoples. His natural sympathy with the oppressed, whether individuals or groups, which we have observed in him from earliest youth, is quickened and deepened by his awareness of the sharp contrast between the past glory of Greece and Italy and their ignominious present. Joseph rightly observes that *Childe Harold* is "as much a political as an antiquarian poem."[11]

The final scene of *Childe Harold's Pilgrimage* is the ocean, which is for Byron the "Type and Symbol of Eternity." The famous apostrophe to the ocean, beginning, "Roll on, thou deep and dark blue Ocean — roll! / Ten thousand fleets sweep over thee in vain;. . .," continues as he contrasts the sea's permanence with empires: "Thy shores are empires, changed in all save thee— / Assyria — Greece — Rome — Carthage — what are they?" And he concludes with eloquence appropriate to the sublimity of ocean:

> Thou glorious mirror, where the Almighty's form
> Glasses itself in tempests; in all time,
> Calm or convulsed — in breeze, or gale, or storm —
> Icing the Pole, or in the torrid clime
> Dark-heaving, — boundless, endless, and sublime —
> The image of Eternity — the throne
> Of the Invisible; even from out thy slime
> The monsters of the deep are made — each Zone
> Obeys thee — thou goest forth, dread, fathomless, alone.

"The fourth canto," writes Calvert, "is Byron's final, complete break with the past. . . .He is from now on committed to truth and reason."[12] What he has written here is intrinsically his own and essentially Byron, and it is uttered with vigor and sincerity. The paradox of Byron is nowhere better exemplified; for, if the subject matter is Romantic, the mode and mood are Augustan. He achieves a harmonious reconciliation of the best qualities of each. "The verse is magnificent because Byron was living magnificently; it is the voice of a great spirit speaking out in intense sincerity."[13]

More recently, Professor Elledge, addressing himself to the primarily non-satiric works of Byron, has written of "the poet's refusal to be restrained by any single world, philosophy, attitude, or mode of conduct. Forever spinning between the poles of dualism and monism, intellect and emotion, flesh and spirit, clay and fire, he represents ... the irreconcilable opposites which are responsible for the 'commotion' of mortal existence."[14]

And Professor McGann, assessing *Childe Harold* as a whole, writes, "In a sense it is Byron's most important work: no other poem contains more information about himself and his ideas, not even *Don Juan*."[15] Even Wordsworth, McGann declares, "in his most sublime moments has not eclipsed the grand conclusion of Byron's poem, with its comprehensive presentation of the greatness and the littleness, the glory and the insignificance of man, his works, and his days."[16]

I agree with Rutherford's wise appraisal of Canto IV as essentially transitional in nature. For years Byron had been seeking a poetic form and convention suitable to the expression of his complex nature. Now he is approaching a more authentic and vital idiom for the reflection of his more personal everyday feelings. Now "...his long apprenticeship was nearly over, and with *Beppo* we pass from the realm of largely vain experiment ... into that of positive achievement and great poetry."[17]

II Beppo

Of great importance to the literary future of Byron was the juncture, late in August, of an amusing Venetian story, which Byron heard from Signor Segati, and of John Hookham Frere's *Whistlecraft,* which was then brought to Byron's attention. Frere had employed the flexible *ottava rima* in his mock-heroic satirical poem modeled after the Italian burlesque manner and mode of Luigi Pulci, Francesco Berni, and Giambattista Casti.[18] Byron found this serio-comic mood, colloquial style, and versatile meter a most appropriate vehicle for the amusing story of Venetian manners and easy morals. And, more important, he found the serio-comic manner and mode ideally suited to the exhilarating sense he was now beginning to feel of emancipation from British decorum and his own earlier *Childe Harold* sentiment and melancholy.[19] By

October 10 he had finished *Beppo,* his poetic experiment in the Italian burlesque mode.

Exhilarated by the novelty, excitement, and freedom of Venetian life, Byron began to view his own recent *Childe Harold* mood of melancholy, remorse, and defiant pride with amused objectivity. After finishing the original version of *Manfred,* Byron wrote Murray, "It is too much in my old style; . . . I certainly am a devil of a mannerist, and must leave off. . .[20]" His mood in 1817, vastly different from that of 1816, is tellingly revealed in a letter to his publisher after the publication of *Beppo:* "It will show them that I can write cheerfully, and repel the charge of monotony and mannerism."[21] And, although he revised *Manfred* in 1817 and wrote the fourth canto of *Childe Harold,* Byron is now fundamentally changed, both as man and poet.

Byron's entire creative life is a pilgrimage in quest of self-realization. As Calvert wisely discerns, his artistic development is not merely a record of fluctuating influences and experimental search for poetic form; it is instead, the gradual growth of a personality. In one sense, his development is a self-discovery of what is latent within him; but, in a more important sense, it is a self-creation: "He had first of all to create himself."[22]

The new image of himself is one in which his strong drive to emotional self-expression and his reasoned poetic will, heretofore separated, are harmoniously integrated. What Joseph calls Byron's "two master impulses" — his need to recreate experience imaginatively and to comment on experience satirically, until now pulling him in divergent directions — meet and join forces in artistic congruity.[23] He can still write out of his *estro* with feeling, but he can now laugh at himself with impunity. This attractive side of the many-faceted Byron — his social personality familiar to his intimates — the poet had felt constrained to exclude from his serious work. The urbane, *bon vivant,* man-of-the-world aspect of Byron's personality is never allowed free rein in his poetry until *Beppo* and *Don Juan.*

Miss Boyd has pointed out the relevancy and importance of Byron's letter-writing style to his new poetic vein. Byron's letters (significantly, most of his correspondents were men) are among the most spirited and richly varied letters in the language. Pervaded by a delightful combination of comic vision and common sense, his letters are racy, witty, colloquial, conversational. Likewise, his style of talk, like that of his letter writing, was brilliant, vivacious, anecdotal, stuffed with his prejudices and predilections of all kinds, and always frankly and disarmingly personal. The distinctive qualities of Byron's letters and conversation were soon to appear in his poetry.[24]

All these salutary factors of liberating circumstance, relaxed mood, self-discovery, and artistic maturity converged at the appropriate time. The comic vision and colloquial style of his prose and conversation were fully developed and ready. All that was needed was, in Rutherford's inspired phrase, "a catalyst ... to precipitate them into poetry."[25]

John Hookham Frere's *Whistlecraft,* burlesquing the Arthurian legend in colloquial English and the Pulcian *ottava rima,* was the necessary agent. From *Whistlecraft,* in September of 1817, Byron learned how to adapt the mood and manner of the Italian "burlesque" poets, Pulci, Berni, and Casti, to the English language and to exploit to the full the versatile qualities of his own letters and conversation. "The colloquial verve and gaiety of Frere's verses," writes Miss Boyd, "set a new tune ringing in his head."[26] He began immediately his poetic experiment in the congenial new mode — serio-comic, conversational, digressive, ironic; finished it in October; and named it *Beppo.*

The style of *Beppo* is as near prose as poetry can be, allowing Byron to speak in his natural voice, as if writing a letter, racy, gay, witty, and in the urbane tone and idiom of a sophisticated man of the world. The *ottava rima* vehicle provides him ample narrative room for dramatic characterization and action, as well as for unlimited digressive comment.[27] Altogether exorcised from *Beppo* is the lugubrious spirit of the Byronic Hero with his self-pity, pride, and pessimism. The earlier hero-protagonist is making way for the poet-narrator relationship to be achieved in *Don Juan.*

The story of *Beppo* is slight, a mere peg on which to hang the poet's digressions. The amusing and scandalous Venetian anecdote which Byron heard from Signor Segati provides the narrative element. Beppo, a Venetian merchant, reappears during the Carnival after years of Turkish captivity to find that his wife, Laura, has taken the Count as her lover. He discloses his identity, reunites with his wife, and befriends the Count. The racy tale, comparable with the licentious *ottava rima* stories of Casti's *Novelle Galanti,* occupies very few of the ninety-nine stanzas. Around and in and out of this slender narrative fabric the narrator's whimsical digressions and ironic comment flash like summer heat lightning. With amused tolerance the poet allows his digressive comment to play over the vanities, trivialities, and immoralities of Venetian life:

> 'Tis known, at least it should be, that throughout
>   All countries of the Catholic persuasion,
> Some weeks before Shrove Tuesday comes about,
>   The people take their fill of recreation,
> And buy repentance, ere they grow devout,
>   However high their rank, or low their station,
> With fiddling, feasting, dancing, drinking, masquing,
> And other things which may be had for asking.   3 1-2

One of his favorite themes for digressive comment is the sharp contrast between Italy and England on which he rings the changes, much to the latter's disadvantage. The social and political defects of England are unobtrusively and humorously exposed with special stress on the strictness of the moral code. He prefers the easy morals of the Italians, as exemplified by Laura:

> And Laura waited long, and wept a little,
>   And thought of wearing weeds, as well she might;
> She almost lost all appetite for victual,
>   And could not sleep with ease alone at night;
> She deemed the window-frames and shutters brittle
>   Against a daring housebreaker or sprite,
> And so she thought it prudent to connect her   4
> With a vice-husband, *chiefly* to *protect her.*

Sexuality — a major theme in *Beppo,* as Marshall observes — is not treated seriously.[28] In fact, as Rutherford wisely points out, *Beppo* is the "rare and paradoxical phenomenon of a great satire based not on morality but immorality," which depends for its success on Byron's deliberate exclusion of his profounder moral attitudes and convictions about man and society. Later, and most notably in *Don Juan,* he transcends the limitations of this frivolous cynicism in the clear vision of his serio-comic world-view. But, now, with zest and infectious enthusiasm he chooses to "hymn adultery," reveal the relativism of moral codes, celebrate sensual pleasure as the *summum bonum* of civilized man, and convey the sheer "*fun* of being alive and sinning" or of living a normal life of ordinary activities like eating, drinking, talking, and making love. So vigorous is his vitality and so ingratiating his humor that the effect is one of affirmation, not of negation.[29]

Beppo is a trial-piece for *Don Juan.* Or, like an overture to an opera, it states in miniature most of the essentials of mode and manner of the major work — alternation of narration and digression, separation of hero and narrator, and *ottava rima* virtuosity. Conspicuously lacking, however, are the grand sweep and underlying deep seriousness of Byron's epic satire.

Byron and Hobhouse spent a delightful fall at La Mira, where the poet added to the fourth canto of *Childe Harold* and where his friend worked on his *Historical Notes* to the poem. By November the two friends, back in Venice, were writing, attending the opera and *conversazione;* riding horseback on the Lido sands; swimming; and talking endlessly. For Byron, there was the added fillip of a new inamorata, Margarita Cogni, who was rivaling Marianna in his affections. Margarita, a baker's wife, was tall, darkly beautiful, leonine, passionate, fiercely possessive — one of the "fine animals" of Byron's ambivalent tastes in women.

On January 8, 1818, Hobhouse bade farewell to his closest friend and left for England, taking with him the fourth canto of *Childe Harold.* Little did he realize that Byron had discovered in *Beppo* his true bent and that henceforth, freed from mannerism and restraint, Byron would write his most original and important poetic works in this fresh, realistic, serio-comic mood and style.

CHAPTER 8

1818–1821

Don Juan *and Poetic Dramas*

A LTHOUGH Byron had entered enthusiastically and without inhibition into the Carnival and although he had abandoned himself strenuously to every dissipation, he had not stopped his literary work. On January 19 he dispatched *Beppo* to Murray with the instruction to print it anonymously. His thirtieth birthday, January 22, passed uneventfully, except that he met, for the first time, at the Albrizzi *conversazione,* the pretty young Countess Teresa Guiccioli; but this very casual meeting made very little impression on either of them. Murray published *Beppo* on February 28; its authorship was at once recognized, and Jeffrey praised its good-natured satire in the *Edinburgh Review.*

The Carnival over, Byron continued his excessive sexual indulgence with the middle- and lower-class Venetian women whom he found to be such "fine animals" — voluptuous, passionate, aggressive, grossly sensual, and unrestrained. His favorite was obstreperous, possessive Margarita Cogni, his latest *amica,* who had effectively dispossessed Marianna Segati. Byron exchanged his cramped quarters over the draper's shop for the magnificent Palazzo Mocenigo on the Grand Canal, which he leased for three years. Despite fourteen servants, and the canal-level ground floor given over to an increasing menagerie of animal pets including monkeys and dogs, there was ample room in the upper three floors of the spacious palazzo for the veritable harem of Venetian women who came and went through the Mocenigo, ruled over by the fiercely jealous "Fornarina" — Margarita Cogni. By this time Byron's promiscuities had become notorious in Venice, and rumors of his extravagant dissipations had reached even England.

100

This information was disquieting for the Shelleys and Claire Clairmont who were leaving for Italy and bringing with them Byron's natural daughter who had been baptized Clara Allegra Byron. Claire had agreed, in spite of Shelley's disapproval, to Byron's terms for the future of Allegra: he was to support and educate the child, have sole authority over her, but have nothing to do with the mother. When the Shelley party arrived in Milan in April, little Allegra was sent about the first of May to Venice in the charge of a Swiss nurse. The pretty, fair-haired, blue-eyed, lively, and intelligent little girl was soon the favorite of all and the pride of her "Papa."

In spite of the debilitation of excessive love-making and of obesity, because of the relaxation of his strict dieting regimen, Byron was continuing his writing. Rising late each day, as was his wont, he devoted the late afternoon to riding horseback on the Lido or to swimming, and the evenings to love-making. But, after all was finally quiet in the spacious rooms of the great palazzo, Byron wrote late into the night. While awaiting news of the reception of *Childe Harold,* Canto IV, published by Murray on April 28, Byron seems to have begun further efforts in the serio-comic mood of *Beppo* as early as July, for he wrote Murray on July 10 that he had "two Stories, one serious and one ludicrous (*a la Beppo*), not yet finished, and in no hurry to be so."[1] The "serious" one was *Mazeppa,* a Cossack verse tale; the latter was *Don Juan,* Canto I. When Shelley, at Claire's urging, visited Byron on August 22 at the Mocenigo palace, the warm and mutually stimulating reunion — one later recorded in Shelley's poetic dialogue, *Julian and Maddalo* — gave Shelley opportunity to express his admiration for Byron's new style and mood in *Don Juan.*

I Don Juan *Begun*

On September 19 Byron wrote Moore that he had finished the first canto of a poem in the *Beppo* manner. "It is called *Don Juan,* and is meant to be a little quietly facetious upon everything."[2] Wanting a hero, and not finding in his era a "true one," he would "therefore take our ancient friend Don Juan...." Part of the fun was Byron's deliberate Englishing of the Spanish Don's name to make it rhyme with "new one" and "true one." Familiar with the Don Juan legend, Byron deliberately altered the traditional Don's character and made him the innocent victim of womankind, "more sinned against than sinning," a handsome, winsome, beloved rogue, like Fielding's Tom Jones. In the young Don Juan's mother, Donna Inez, Byron painted a thinly disguised portrait of Lady Byron.

The freedom of the *ottava rima* allowed Byron not only to tell conversationally the hilarious bedroom escapade of Don Juan and Donna Julia but also to intersperse random animadversions and whimsical digressions on anything under the sun. He dedicated *Don Juan* in "good, simple, savage verse" to England's Poet-Laureate, Southey, as a former Liberal who had turned apostate "Tory, ultra-Julian," and as one who had circulated stories in England to the effect that Byron and Shelley had formed a "League of Incest" with Mary and Claire in Switzerland. Canto I of *Don Juan,* together with *Mazeppa,* Byron sent to Murray in November and soon thereafter began with relish Canto II telling of Juan's sea voyage, shipwreck, and idyllic romance with Haidée.

Early in the new year of 1819 Byron's English "committee" of literary advisers — Hobhouse, Douglas Kinnaird, Scrope Davies, and John Hookham Frere — forwarded their reaction to *Don Juan* to Byron in a long letter from Hobhouse. Admiring its genius, wit, and satire, they were alarmed by its "licentiousness," "indecency," "flings at religion," indiscriminate attacks on "other worthy writers of the day," and satire of Lady Byron. They felt that Byron was not aware of the marked change in British moral temper which had followed the moral laxity of the Regency period.[3] Fearing for Byron's literary reputation, they urged the suppression of *Don Juan.*[4]

Byron at first consented to the publication of a few copies for private circulation, but he warned Murray that eventually "we will circumvent" cautious advisers — "my cursed puritanical committee." If his friends had told him the poetry was bad, he would have acquiesced; "but they say the contrary, and then talk to me about morality. . . .I maintain that it is the most moral of poems; but if people won't discover the moral, that is their fault, not mine."[5] But, after the Carnival, Byron was resolved that *Don Juan* must be published publicly, if anonymously: "You shan't make *Canticles* of my Cantos. The poem will please if it is lively; if it is stupid, it will fail; but I will have none of your damned cutting and slashing."[6]

II *Byron and Teresa Guiccioli*

By the beginning of April, 1819, Byron, weary of debauchery, resolved to reform his way of life. Though his mind was as acute as ever and his creative powers at the top of their bent, he was physically and emotionally exhausted. He had fired the Fornarina and had also rid himself of his miscellaneous harem. Seeking a change, he went one evening to the Countess Benzoni's *conversazione.* About midnight the door opened and a beautiful young girl of nineteen appeared — the Countess Teresa Guiccioli, escorted by her husband of one year, Count Alessandro Guiccioli, fifty-eight years of age. Byron may not have remembered meeting her very casually the year before, but her beauty was not lost upon him now — her auburn curls, large lovely eyes, voluptuous face, beautifully shaped shoulders and arms, and abundant bosom. She, on her part, was immediately intrigued by the classic beauty of Byron's face, his ineffable smile, and the melody of his voice. Presented by the Countess Benzoni as "Peer of England and its greatest poet," Byron was charmed by Teresa's knowledge of Dante and Petrarch and by her enthusiasm for Classical Italian literature. Perhaps both Byron and Teresa felt that fate had brought them together, but Teresa was so convinced of it that she later wrote in her *Vie de Lord Byron en Italie* that "the effect of this meeting was the seal of the destiny of their hearts."[7]

The two met clandestinely the next day at Byron's private *casino;* thereafter, Byron became, willy-nilly, virtually Teresa's *cavalier servente.* According to the code of *serventismo,* it was customary and desirable for a married woman to have a *relazione,* or "friendship," with a lover, or *amico,* who served his *dama* according to the traditions of "courtly love"; and the husband theoretically was not to be jealous. Though Byron rankled under his role, he accepted it and enjoyed to the full ten blissful days until Count Guiccioli returned with his wife to Ravenna.

After Teresa had gone, Byron was as disconsolate as a youth in the agonies of his first passion. He began writing tender love letters to her in Italian — letters quite the antithesis of his familiar manly and realistic letters to his English correspondents: "You sometimes tell me that I have been your *first* real love — and I assure you that you shall be my last Passion. . . .Before I knew you — I felt an interest in many women, but never in one only. Now I love *you,* there is no other woman in the world for me." This was to be, whether he fully realized it or not, his "Last Attachment" — one so beautifully chronicled by the Marchesa Iris Origo.[8]

At Ravenna, Teresa grew ill and urged her lover to come to her. In Venice, Byron postponed his departure because of his conflict over his attachment to Teresa and his reluctance to commit himself to a permanent liaison. Finally, Byron left on June 1 for Ravenna, arrived on June 10, and took a room in the Albergo Imperiale near the tomb of Dante. Byron's official host at Ravenna was the Count Giuseppe Alborghetti, Secretary General of the Government of the Lower Romagna, a cultivated man of great influence and authority in the region. He became Byron's behind-the-scenes aider and abettor throughout the English peer's entire Ravenna period.[9]

Byron found himself more passionately in love than ever with Teresa, but at first her illness prevented an intimate reunion. By mid-June she was well enough to accompany Byron on a carriage ride in the pine forest that stretched along the seashore southward toward Rimini. Inspired by this romantic literary pilgrimage, Byron began *The Prophecy of Dante,* a tribute to the great poet and an appeal to the Italians to throw off the Austrian yoke. Another day, as Teresa's health improved, they read together the story of Paolo and Francesca from the *Inferno* and felt the situation quite like their own. They made the most of their precarious opportunities for furtive love-making in the Palazzo Guiccioli, almost under the Count's nose; but they preserved the outward conventions of *serventismo* under which Byron rankled. Teresa grew rapidly better, chiefly owing to the gentle ministrations of her lover whose daily amatory "attentions" were the best therapy for her largely psychosomatic illness.[10] When the taciturn Count took Teresa with him to his property in Bologna on August 9, Byron followed the next day.

Meanwhile, in England Murray had published *Mazeppa* in June. And on July 15, 1819, he cautiously issued the first two cantos of *Don Juan* without the name of author or publisher. The outrage and denunciation of the British to *Don Juan* exceeded all the fearful expectations of Byron's "puritanical committee." Byron was accused — as his friends had feared — of blasphemy, immorality, obscenity, slander, and every other sin; indeed, the hostile reception of his mock-heroic epic satire was almost without parallel.[11] But Byron knew he was on the right track and had found his true forte.

In reply to Murray's question about his plan for *Don Juan,* Byron answered: "I *have* no plan — I *had* no plan. . . .Why, Man, the Soul of such writing is its licence; at least the *liberty* of that *licence.* . . . You are too earnest and eager about a work never intended to be serious. Do you suppose that I could have any intention but to giggle and make giggle?"[12]

But, as I have already noted, Byron did not realize that his every movement was being closely scrutinized by the Austrian secret police, who regarded him as a dangerous liberal and as a friend of Italian intransigents in the Romagna. From time to time Byron's thoughts turned restlessly to the struggle for political reform being waged in England. In a period of ruthless repression, in which a bloody affair such as the "Manchester Massacre" of 1819 could take place, Byron was resolved that he would return to England to "join-up" if it came to revolution.

During a temporary absence of Teresa from Bologna, Byron wandered about the empty rooms of the Guiccioli palace and, finding a copy of Madame de Staël's *Corinne,* one of Teresa's favorite novels, he wrote in the flyleaf his most tender love-letter: "My dear Teresa, — I have read this book in your garden; — my love, you were absent, or else I could not have read it. It is a favourite book of yours, and the writer was a friend of mine. You will not understand these English words, and *others* will not understand them — which is the reason I have not scrawled them in Italian. But you will recognise the handwriting of him who passionately loved you, and you will divine that, over a book which was yours, he could only think of love. In that word, beautiful in all languages, but most so in yours — *Amor mio* — is comprised my existence here and hereafter. ... My destiny rests with you ..."[13]

Teresa's illness having conveniently returned, she told the Count she must return to Venice to secure Dr. Aglietti's care and that Byron would obligingly accompany her. They made an idyllic, leisurely carriage journey, stopping on the way at Arqua to visit the grave of Petrarch; and by September 20 they were delightfully established under one roof at Byron's summer place, La Mira. Byron resumed his congenial habit of breakfasting at two in the afternoon, playing in the garden with Allegra, riding with Teresa at sunset, and making love in the evening. Again, late at night, he was at his desk to work on a third canto of *Don Juan.* Early in October Byron was delighted with a visit from Thomas Moore, one of the companions of his happy bachelor years in London. Moore admired the passion, wit, and vigor of the new stanzas of *Don Juan*. Before Moore left, Byron gave him the manuscript of his "Memoirs" not to be published during his lifetime and containing, among other things, a detailed account of his marriage. These were the "Memoirs" subsequently sold to Murray and later destroyed in Murray's office after Byron's death.[14]

At the end of October Count Guiccioli came to Venice to take his wife home to Ravenna. He came armed with a list of twenty-five maxims or rules, by which his wife was henceforth to govern her conduct. But the spirited Teresa, who spurned them completely, maintained she would return to Ravenna only if her *amico* accompanied her. Both husband and wife unyielding, and the battle in Byron's palace between them raged for ten days. Finally, she consented to go with her husband, but only with the understanding that her lover might again join her in Ravenna.[15]

Alone and despondent, Byron now gave serious consideration to returning to England with Allegra. While he waited and debated, he found relief in relating in *Don Juan* the idyllic love of Juan and Haidée. But now his affair with Teresa took a new twist as her father, Count Ruggero Gamba, alarmed by his daughter's relapse into illness — her psychosomatic indisposition having conveniently returned — wrote Byron from Filetto, his country house near Ravenna, begging him to rejoin the ailing Teresa.[16] With relief and resignation Byron complied; when he arrived at Ravenna on Christmas Eve, he was warmly welcomed by Teresa and her father.

III   Cavalier Servente

Now, at the beginning of 1820, Byron was willy-nilly, Teresa's acknowledged *cavalier servente*. He was therefore cordially received by her family and friends, and politely tolerated by her suave, calculating, strong-willed husband, Count Guiccioli. Byron was the honored guest at a round of social affairs followed by the Carnival, in the midst of which he was thoughtful enough to write a kind letter to Lady Byron urging her to peruse his "Memoirs" sent by Moore to England and to "mark any part or parts that do not appear to coincide with the truth."[17] Significantly, the adamant Lady Byron refused to read the "Memoirs."

Early in January the unfathomable Count Guiccioli offered to rent to Byron the upper floor of the spacious Palazzo Guiccioli. Soon Teresa's *amico* was settled under the same roof with her, and a pleasant routine of riding in the pincta, attending the theater, and love-making was established which permitted Byron to return to poetic expression. In mid-February, undeterred by the extravagant British disapproval of the first installment of his satire, he sent Murray the third and fourth cantos of *Don Juan.*

He was annoyed by the news that Hobhouse had been arrested for writing a pamphlet deemed by the House of Commons a breach of privilege, and he mistakenly assumed that his friend had deserted the Whigs to consort with the Westminster Reformers. As Marchand points out, it is a further example of Byron's paradoxical liberalism versus his deep-grained aristocratic bent that, like Carlyle and other nineteenth-century intellectuals, he sympathized with the cause of the oppressed common people but always envisioned their deliverance by aristocratic leaders of liberal leaning.[18] Byron failed to appreciate the fact that Hobhouse had made genuine sacrifices for the principles of constitutional government and that the Westminster Reformers were now the liberal party in England rather than the pusillanimous Whigs.[19]

In the spring of 1820 Byron began to take a serious interest in Italian politics — and especially in the insurrectionary movement looking toward the overthrow of the Austrian overlordship. Moreover, Byron and Count Ruggero Gamba were mutually attracted by their congenial liberal interests. Count Gamba, Teresa's father, was an enthusiastic Italian patriot and influential leader in the Carbonari, a secret revolutionary society. In April Byron wrote Kinnaird and Murray of revolutionary incitements in the Romagna. He expected "a *row* here in a short time"; and, although he doubted the success of the insurrectionists because they lacked union, he applauded their "cause." Meanwhile, Byron's literary endeavors bore a relationship to his political interests; for he was at work on a poetic drama, the tragedy of *Marino Faliero,* Doge of Venice.

IV *Political Dramas*

In *Beppo* Byron had found the poetic medium best suited to his genius — the serio-comic mood and mode of the Italian comic-epic writers in *ottava rima.* But, unfortunately, he did not at first devote himself exclusively to his new experimental style. Rutherford is right in lamenting Byron's slowness in recognizing the superlative importance of his new poetic vehicle.[20] After finishing *Beppo,* he had returned to *Childe Harold,* Canto IV, written the *Ode to Venice,* and composed another verse-tale, *Mazeppa.* Now, early in 1820, discouraged by the reception of *Don Juan,* Cantos I and II, and uncertain about its future, Byron turned his attention to non-satiric writing and devoted most of his creative effort throughout 1820 and 1821 to poetic drama. Between April and July of 1820 he wrote *Marino Faliero,* the first and perhaps the best of his political dramas modeled on Classical principle. By the end of 1821 he had written three such dramas.

Byron's interest in the drama, both Classical and Shakespearian, had begun very early, but with a steadily growing preference for the Classical. During Harrow and Cambridge days he had frequently taken part in amateur theatricals. Upon invitation, he wrote the poetic *Address* for the opening of the rebuilt Drury Lane Theatre in 1812 and was elected to the subcommittee of the Drury Lane Board of Managers in 1814. He devoted his best efforts to securing good plays and recruiting excellent actors for the Drury Lane but with discouraging results as far as the plays were concerned. He was very well aware of the low state of the English stage, deeply deplored it, and was predisposed to address his best efforts to its reformation.

When he tried his hand at poetic drama in 1820, he modeled his plays after Classical principles and intended them definitely as closet drama "for the reader, not for the stage." He wished to appeal not to the theater crowd but to the élite in taste and judgment. His avowed desire was to reform the English stage, cryingly needed in Byron's time, and to revive serious drama. The English theater had degenerated since Shakespeare's day, and the contemporary drama was structurally loose, thematically weak, and absurdly bombastic. The unified, coherent, organic form of Classic drama appealed strongly to Byron. In his search for form in poetic drama he rejected, therefore, the Gothic mode approximated in his own earlier *Manfred* and found his congenial examples in the ancient Greek, neo-Classical French, and contemporary Italian, especially in Alfieri, to whose Classical theory and practice Byron was chiefly indebted. Alfieri's tragedies, patterned after French neo-Classical models and observing the Unities, supplied Byron with examples of both mode and theme for his political dramas, *Marino Faliero, The Two Foscari,* and *Sardanapalus.*[21]

The political implications of *Marino Faliero* are conspicuous. It was written during the period of Byron's increasing involvement in the revolutionary Italian Carbonari movement and at the time that he was growing increasingly distrustful of the efforts of the "Reformers" at home in England. Faliero, the protagonist, Doge of Venice, first honored and then disgraced by his peers, leads a rebellion, is betrayed, and decapitated on the "Giant Stairs" of the Ducal Palace. The play, according to E. D. H. Johnson, thus reflects Byron's own inner conflicts as an aristocrat-revolutionary who loved liberty but distrusted the mob.[22]

The other Venetian tragedy, *The Two Foscari,* restates the same theme, as Joseph demonstrates; but the conflicting claims of country and class loyalty which warred within Faliero are divided between father and son. Intense love of his native Venice compels the young man to sacrifice himself; the absolute demands of the aristocratic hierarchy claim the allegiance of his aged father, the Doge. "Nowhere does he [Byron] show more clearly," writes Joseph, "the division between his desire for simple freedom and natural justice and his feeling that there is a necessary authority"[23]

For *Sardanapalus* Byron moves to Assyrian history and the tragic downfall of the humane and sybaritic King of Nineveh. Sardanapalus is a benevolent voluptuary whose leniency encourages rebellion as surely as Faliero's impassioned violence. The Assyrian king is an enlightened ruler whom Byron conceives as "brave" and willing to yield his life in the best interest of his subjects. In temperament, humaneness, and sacrificial courage, Sardanapalus would suggest Byron's ideal of conduct.

In these three political dramas Byron, in Calvert's view, comes close to the spirit of the Greeks. If these works failed to reform the English stage and to establish an English Classic tradition, it is chiefly because they appeared at the height of the Romantic period and, also, were more Continental and Italianate in spirit than native.[24] Whether *Marino Faliero,* as Rutherford feels, or *Sardanapalus,* Joseph's preference, is the high point of Byron's efforts in Classical drama, all critics can agree that the dramas represent another step in Byron's indefatigable search for appropriate poetic forms. Byron is to be commended for pioneering in his time in the continuing effort from Shakespeare's day to the present to reestablish poetic drama "on a workable contemporary basis." Byron, like Eliot and Yeats of the present century, "saw the need to rethink the whole question of dramatic expression and find new models for it; like his successors, he deserves credit for it, regardless of the success or failure of individual plays."[25]

V The Carbonari Movement

In mid-May, 1820, came a complete reversal on the part of Count Guiccioli in his attitude toward Byron. Hitherto enigmatically tolerant of his wife's lover, he now turned upon Byron and informed him that his presence in the Palazzo Guiccioli was no longer desired. Byron now counseled Teresa, who threatened to separate from the Count and go to her father, to remain with her husband; and he offered to withdraw. Byron's chivalrous offer was genuine, if conventional, believes the Marchesa Origo.[26] Meanwhile, Count Gamba, persuaded of the justice of his daughter's cause and the iniquities of her tyrannical husband, appealed to the Pope for a decree of separation. Count Gamba had influential friends close to Pope Pius VII, and Count Giuseppe Alborghetti used his influence with the Cardinal Malvasia in behalf of Teresa and Byron.[27] While the separation was pending, Byron wrote Teresa to reassure her that he would never abandon her: "...my love — my duty — my honour — all these and everything should make me forever what I am *now,* your lover friend and (when circumstances permit) your *husband.*"[28]

In mid-July the news arrived that the Pope had granted a decree of separation to Teresa, and Count Gamba took his daughter to his country house at Filetto. Byron, deprived of frequent access to his love — the decree provided that Teresa must live under her parental roof — remained in his apartments in the Guiccioli palace in Ravenna. But his letters to Teresa convey the attitude of a devoted and solicitous husband more than that of a *cavalier servente.* For a month the two lovers were deprived of the love-making which had become such a congenial part of their lives. But Byron continued his enormous correspondence and also finished and sent Murray by mid-August his five-act historical drama, *Marino Faliero.*

At this time Byron first met Teresa's charming brother, Pietro Gamba, fresh from his studies in Rome, an ardent Italian patriot, and, like his father, a leader of the Carbonari movement in the Romagna. Byron was immediately attracted to the youthful Pietro, who was about a year younger than his sister; and, since the attraction was mutual, a lasting friendship was cemented. Byron, soon drawn into the secret Carbonari activities of the region, became an honorary "Capo" or chief of the lowest, or workmen's order, of the Carbonari called "Turbo" or mob. The revolutionaries accorded him deference as an aristocratic English liberal, and he supplied them with arms. Accordingly, Byron's activities were increasingly scrutinized by the Austrian secret police and his letters were opened.

To get Allegra out of the summer heat and to be near Teresa, Byron rented a country house near the Casa Gamba at Filetto. In mid-August Byron and Teresa were reunited, and Byron became a frequent and welcome visitor at the spacious country house of the Gambas[29] who accepted him with warm affection as one of the family. The admired English peer was, moreover, ever more deeply embroiled in the secret Carbonari activities of the Gambas; in fact, according to the Marchesa Origo, some fifteen thousand members of the secret revolutionary society were in the Romagna at this time.[30] An uprising was planned for early September, and Byron was suspected of furnishing money and supplies. Some of the conspirators were arrested, others fled the Romagna, but the Gambas and Byron were unmolested. Meanwhile, the Carbonari of the Romagna waited hopefully on the outcome of the expected revolution in Naples. But the news, filtering through from Europe, was not reassuring; the leading European powers meeting in the Congress at Troppau had reaffirmed their right to suppress internal revolutions and had given Austria the right to crush the Neapolitan revolution in Italy.[31]

The year 1821 opened with heady prospects of revolutionary activity in Naples. The hope that the Neapolitans might resist the Austrians prompted Byron to write a stirring address to the insurgents in Naples promising generous financial aid and volunteering his personal services in behalf of a liberated Italy. Likewise, he began a journal of his Ravenna experiences and personal reflections; and he drafted plans for another poetic drama, the tragedy of *Sardanapalus;* gave thought to a metaphysical drama to be called *Cain;* and plunged into the literary-critical fray raging in England over the merits of Pope, his own poetic idol. On February 13 he sent Murray a fifty-five-page letter *On the Rev. W. L. Bowles' Strictures on the Life and Writings of Pope* which was published shortly thereafter in pamphlet form. But that Byron's *chef d'oeuvre* was still *Don Juan* is indicated by his writing Murray that his epic satire was only just begun and by his facetiously outlining his plan for its continuation. He meant to take his Don on a tour of Europe in order to ridicule the societies of the several countries in turn, but he was uncertain whether "to make him end in Hell, or in an unhappy marriage, not knowing which would be the severest."[32]

Concerned for Allegra's safety should revolution break out in the Romagna, Byron put his four-year-old daughter in the school for girls in the convent of Bagnacavallo near Ravenna. Although this action brought a shocked protest from Claire, Byron declared that he desired his daughter to be a Roman Catholic which he regarded as the "best" and "oldest" branch of Christianity. In April Shelley wrote Byron of the death of Keats in Rome, and about the same time came the keenly disappointing news of the failure of the Neapolitan revolt against the Austrians. Byron's gloom deepened when he learned from Murray of the presentation against Byron's explicit wishes of *Marino Faliero* at the Drury Lane in May.

However, he was greatly encouraged in May, 1821, by the high praise accorded his *Don Juan* in an anonymous pamphlet, *Letter to the Right Hon. Lord Byron* by "John Bull," who has recently been identified by Alan Strout as Sir Walter Scott's son-in-law, John Gibson Lockhart.[33] This publication was one of the few examples of contemporary critical recognition that Byron had found in *Don Juan* his true forte and was at the top of his bent.[34] Paradoxically enough, it was at this very time of exultation over "John Bull's" appreciation of *Don Juan* that Byron was persuaded by Teresa to discontinue his epic satire. She had been distressed by its cynical treatment of love ever since she had read the French translation the preceding autumn, and she also felt that the work was bringing Byron into disrepute. Reluctantly, Byron agreed not to resume *Don Juan* until she authorized his doing so.

Prophetic of a major chapter yet to come in Byron's life was his excitement over the news of the outbreak in March, 1821, of the Greek War of Independence. When the news reached him belatedly in June, Byron wrote Moore: "The Greeks! what think you? They are my old acquaintances — but what to think I know not. Let us hope howsomever."[35] On July 10, without warning, Pietro Gamba was arrested as a conspirator against the state and expelled from its borders. He and his father, Count Gamba, both exiled, went first to Bologna and then to Florence.

Teresa remained at Ravenna with Byron until July 25 when with his aid she made her escape to Florence. Staying on in the Palazzo Guiccioli, Byron labored now on his first serious poetic exploration of the problems of evil, death, and immortality in his metaphysical drama, *Cain.* The relationship of these problems to predestination and free will had continued to haunt Byron since his Calvinistic training in childhood. The protagonist Cain is, again, another autobiographical self-portrait of Byron as "intellectual rebel and rationalistic skeptic."[36]

VI *"Metaphysical" Drama:* Cain

Cain, written in 1821 immediately after *The Two Foscari,* represents a marked shift in Byron's interest from "politics to theology," society to cosmos. A Biblical play in language and matter, it is patterned after the Medieval mystery plays rather than the Classical drama. Like the uninhibited mystery plays, *Cain* freely interprets and revises the biblical materials. Its sources are the Old Testament and the philosophy of the Age of Reason, both of which were familiar and congenial to Byron, Calvinist-trained, a Deist, and an intellectual rebel. In his Preface to *Cain* Byron named among his sources Genesis, Solomon Gessner's *Der Tod Abeles,* and Georges Cuvier's notions of catastrophism. He acknowledged, elsewhere, that his treatment of iconoclasm and revolt had its closest parallel in *Paradise Lost.* For the cosmic voyage he had models in Edward Young's *Night Thoughts* and Shelley's *Queen Mab.*

And his ideological antecedents, as Joseph indicates are an amalgam of Calvinism, rejected but ineluctable; Lucretian atomism; Bernard de Fontenelle's plurality of worlds; Pope's Deism; *Vathek's* Pre-Adamism; Comte de Buffon's giants and "organic degeneration"; and Cuvier's cyclical catastrophism. Byron was writing in the brief period between the collapse of the fundamentalist belief in Genesis and the biological and geological synthesis of Charles Lyell and Charles Darwin. His myth, with its sense of cosmic vastness and incomprehensible Deity, is essentially modern.[37]

As Marshall indicates at the beginning of his extended analysis of the theme and structure of *Cain,* the work is chiefly concerned with the conflict between good and evil, a Goethe-like metaphysical encounter between Lucifer and Cain, a second Temptation and Fall. Cain, the protagonist, tries in vain to resolve the conflict between cosmic injustice and his own sense of right. Unable to reconcile the unreason of Abel's sacrifice to a seemingly unjust God, Cain, a logical absolutist, brings the first death into the world.[38]

Byron's works from *Childe Harold* to *Cain* run the gamut from natural benevolism and Romantic pantheism in *Childe Harold* III to the rejection of benevolism in *Manfred* and the expression of evolutionary pessimism in *Cain*. When *Cain* was published in December, 1821, the hue and cry was extreme, the chief charge being blasphemy. But by this time Byron had written a work which, in Rutherford's words, constituted "an attack on Orthodoxy infinitely more effective than the blundering frontal assaults of *Cain* and *Manfred*."[39] This was his magnificent serio-comic satire, *The Vision of Judgment*.

CHAPTER 9

1821–1822 Byron and Shelley: The Vision of Judgment

EARLY in August, 1821, when Shelley visited Byron at Ravenna, he was happy to find his friend remarkably improved in health and spirits, in contrast to his dissipated condition in Venice. This improvement Byron attributed to the redemptive and stimulating influence of Teresa Guiccioli.[1] Shelley was again deeply impressed with Byron's genius in *Don Juan* (Murray had published Cantos III-V in August), every word of which he felt was "pregnant with immortality."[2] After reading Shelley's elegy on Keats, *Adonais,* Byron instructed Murray to omit from his manuscripts all derogatory remarks about Keats, whose *Hyperion* would assure his immortality.

When Shelley returned to Pisa with the commission to find residences there for the Gambas and Byron, he lost no time in taking for Byron the spacious sixteenth-century Casa Lanfranchi on the Lungarno. The Gambas, who moved to Pisa at the beginning of September, expected Byron to join them promptly. But Teresa's lover, always loath to change his residence and to break an established routine, lingered on in the Palazzo Guiccioli where he was finishing *Cain* and composing a "seditious" satire on George IV called "The Irish Avatar." Then Byron's creative genius, despite all the confusion and discord of packing for moving to Pisa, led him to compose the work Marchand considers "the masterpiece of his whole writing career" — *The Vision of Judgment.*[3]

I The Vision of Judgment

The Vision of Judgment, Byron's robust reply to Southey's *A Vision of Judgment* commemorating the death and burial of

George III, is a brilliantly witty, devastatingly funny satire.
Southey's solemn, semi-official, and sycophantic eulogy appeared
in April, 1821. Byron began his *Vision* on May 7, dropped it the
same day, and resumed in mid-September, finishing it on October
4. After a not uncongenial meeting with Southey in 1813, Byron
had been alienated by Southey's malicious gossip about Byron and
the Shelley menage — "League of Incest" — at Geneva and had
retaliated in his Dedication to *Don Juan*. Southey, in his Preface to
his *Vision,* attacked Byron as the leader of the "Satanic School."
Now, in his superb satiric travesty of the Laureate's work, Byron
delivered the final *coup de grâce* to Southey and his inflated *Vision*.

Briefly, Southey's *Vision* relates the arrival of the old and mad
King George at the gate of Heaven where his majestic glance si-
lences his accusers. The Devil and all the former enemies of the
King are hurled down to Hell while the King, absolved of all blame
for his wars and misrule, is received solemnly into Heaven and
beatified. Byron travesties Southey's narrative by presenting a
hilarious burlesque of the decrepit and demented King's arrival at
Heaven's gate, his quizzing by the unimpressed and annoyed St.
Peter, his confrontation with his serious crimes, and his eventual
unobtrusive and unobserved entry into Heaven — all done in a
style, tone, and manner quite antithetical to Southey's.

In the Preface to his *Vision* Byron acknowledges as precedents
for the discourse of "saints, angels, and spiritual persons" on subjects non-serious as well as serious Francisco Quevedo's *Vision*
(1635), Englished in 1815; Henry Fielding's *Journey From This
World to the Next;* Chaucer's *Wife of Bath;* and Swift's *Tale of a
Tub*. But, obviously, Byron needed no model besides Southey's
absurd *Vision* to inspire him.

The several reasons for Byron's spirited rejoinder to Southey are
lucidly summarized by Rutherford.[4] The personal reasons, already
given, were Southey's rumor-mongering and his thinly veiled
accusations of the immorality and Satanism of Byron's works.
Byron, likewise, had critical reasons for his attack on the vulgarity,
apostasy from neo-Classical poetic standards, and system-
mongering of Southey and the Lake Poets. More important than
his critical disapproval, however, was his despite for the political
apostasy of the Poet Laureate who had begun as the exponent of
revolutionary views in his *Wat Tyler* but had become the apostle of
conservative reaction. Byron set out to correct Southey's delib-

erately false historical estimate of George III and to show up Southey as a political renegade and bad poet. Finally, Byron was outraged by Southey's display of religious hypocrisy, pharisaical bigotry, and intolerance. He regarded Southey's gross flattery and sycophantic praise of George III as the quintessence of English *cant* — "cant political, cant poetical, cant religious, cant moral." "There are but two sentiments to which I am constant," he told Lady Blessington, "—a strong love of liberty, and a detestation of cant..."⁵

Conspicuously different from Southey's is Byron's treatment of Satan. Southey's Devil is contemptible, impudent, and grotesque; Byron's Satan is Miltonic — grand, noble, heroic, the peer and fit adversary of Michael, "the leader, as it were," in Rutherford's telling phrase, of "His Celestial Majesty's Opposition." Satan's indictment of George III is deeply serious and just: the carnage of his wars, his tyranny over America and restoration of tyranny on the Continent, and his suppression of the basic liberties of his subjects at home.

> He ever warred with freedom and the free: 3 1-2
>> Nations as men, home subjects, foreign foes,
> So that they uttered the word 'Liberty!'
>> Found George the Third their first opponent...

Turning abruptly from Southey's narrative, Byron annihilates both Southey and his poem with delightful ridicule. The "hearty anti-jacobin," who "had turned his coat — and would have turned his skin," had first "written praises of a Regicide" and then "of all kings whatever" in "much blank verse, and blanker prose, / And more of both than any body knows." And, finally, Byron discovers an inspired and superb ending for his *Vision*. Southey, who has tried to ride into Heaven on the King's coattails, interrupts the trial of the King with his gratuitous recitation of his "Vision" which throws the angelic assembly into such an uproar that the Laureate falls down into his native Lake and King George slips into Heaven unobserved. And Byron concludes: "And when the tumult dwindled to a calm, / I left him practising the hundredth psalm." So Byron completes his satiric immolation of Southey and his *Vision*.

Byron does all this in his "finest, ferocious, Caravaggio style," a spectacular *chiaroscuro* of grand imaginative depictions and brilliant inventive detail. The antithetical contrast in style between Southey's leaden, plodding hexameters and Byron's flexible and versatile octaves is ample testimony to Byron's mastery of his new poetic form. Byron's tone is now gay and flippant, now grave and grimly ironic, always appropriate to the matter, fully exploiting the endless potentialities of the *ottava rima* medium. Though sometimes conversational and casual in digressions or in urbanely deflating Christian mythology, the prevailing tone is in the high style of Milton and Dante; and it is best represented by the encounter and dialogue between the two magnificent peers, Satan and Michael.

Rutherford, who maintains quite persuasively that the *Vision of Judgment* represents the acme of Byron's genius, points to its superiority over *Don Juan* because of the absence of "the intellectual confusion" sometimes present in the latter work. The *Vision* has, he asserts, what *Don Juan* lacks — "a single major target" and a "clearly defined satiric purpose."[6] Byron thinks and writes like a Whig aristocrat whose concept of freedom is simple but vitally important. It means freedom from foreign rule and despots, of speech and political action, and of thought and religion. Byron's "cynical humor and urge to deflate," which are ubiquitous and sometimes indiscriminating in *Don Juan,* are never permitted to "weaken his own beliefs or feelings" invariably concentrated on his single purpose in *The Vision of Judgment* — that of "reversing rogue Southey's."[7]

The result is a completely unified work of art, coherent and compact, esthetically satisfying and at the same time morally profound. Byron's *Vision* has all *Don Juan's* strengths and excellences with none of its weaknesses. *The Vision of Judgment,* Rutherford concludes, is "the supreme example of satire as it could be written by an English poet-aristocrat."[8] In this assessment he agrees with Professor Marchand, Byron's greatest biographer, who regards the *Vision* as "the masterpiece of his whole writing career" and "the rarest distillation of his satiric genius."[9]

II *Byron and Shelley at Pisa*

Neither would Byron be bullied in Pisa by the thinly disguised efforts of the Romagna authorities in the fall of 1821 to get him out of the country as a dangerous "liberal" and "revolutionary." Their strategy to be rid of him by expelling the Gambas had failed.

Pope Pius VII now issued an encyclical against the Carbonari that threatened excommunication for all who remained in the secret society, but Byron knew the Gambas would never cringe or yield. When, by October 29, Byron finally took his reluctant departure from Ravenna, leaving Allegra in the convent at Bagnacavallo, the Tuscan government officials, as well as the Austrian secret police, were apprehensive about the imminent arrival in Pisa of the dangerous *"Signore Inglese"* known to be a "radical" and a "republican."[10]

On November 1 Byron arrived in Pisa, where Shelley was eagerly anticipating his coming, Pietro and Count Gamba were impatiently waiting, and Teresa had been forlornly watching for her lover's appearance for two long months. Byron found the spacious, three-story Casa Lanfranchi on the Lungarno, with its staircase by Michelangelo, quite to his liking, as well as the mild winter climate of Pisa. He resumed his daily visits with Teresa, who was living with her father and brother nearby; and he soon was drawn into a pleasant Pisan circle of English friends which included Percy and Mary Shelley, Edward and Jane Williams, Shelley's cousin Thomas Medwin, and John Taaffe, an Irish expatriate and scholar-writer of sorts. Byron entertained the male members of this group at a weekly dinner in the Casa Lanfranchi, while the envious womenfolk languished at home.

Byron continued his literary activity in full force under the sunshine of Shelley's admiration and Teresa's warm affection. At home in England *Don Juan,* Cantos III-V, had sold tremendously well to a shocked and disapproving public, but Murray hedged and hesitated about publishing *Cain;* he was fearful of the charge of blasphemy. Finally, on December 19, he published *Sardanapalus, The Two Foscari,* and *Cain.* Because the outcry over *Cain* was extraordinary and because blasphemy was alleged, Murray was hesitant to undertake publication of Byron's latest metaphysical drama, *Heaven and Earth.* Byron, disgusted with "the most timid of God's booksellers," resolved to change publishers.

In mid-January of 1822 a picturesque new figure joined the Pisan circle. The flamboyant Edward John Trelawny, adventurer extraordinary, came to Pisa expressly to meet Shelley and Byron; and to Byron he seemed "the personification of my Corsair." Trelawny at once encouraged Shelley and Williams, as well as Byron, to have boats built for summer sailing on the Bay of Spezia. Subsequently,

Trelawny was commissioned to supervise the construction of an eighteen-foot boat for Shelley and Williams and a handsome schooner for Byron.

Byron found himself quietly and contentedly happy now at Pisa, his relationship with Teresa having taken on the characteristics of a kind of middle-aged domestic tranquility in his thirty-fourth year. But, beneath the surface of Byron's calm existence at Pisa, there was brewing a discord which would eventually damage the mutual accord between Byron and Shelley. Claire Clairmont continued to harass Byron with letters in which she sought to persuade him to remove little Allegra from the convent school, and she was seconded in her appeal by the tactful efforts of Shelley. But Byron was adamant, and Shelley was secretly alienated by Byron's harshness and obduracy toward Claire.

In mid-April, Byron, deeply agitated by the news of Allegra's illness, hurriedly dispatched the best medical care available; but the little girl died on April 20. Byron arranged for the shipping of the body of his little daughter to England to be buried in Harrow Church. Desolated, Byron wrote the sad news to the Shelleys, who had taken a house across from Lerici on the Bay of Spezia. When Claire learned of her loss from the Shelleys, she at first was stunned; then she wrote Byron a letter of severe condemnation for his treatment of her and Allegra.

In the preceding August Shelley had taken it upon himself to invite Leigh Hunt, in the name of Byron, to come to Pisa and to join in the editorship of a literary periodical. Now, in July, nearly a year later, Hunt arrived with his family and was established with Shelley's help in the ground floor apartments of the Casa Lanfranchi. The relationship between Byron and Hunt was never cordial; Byron merely tolerated Hunt, who sought to please his noble benefactor; and he was contemptuous of Hunt's straight-laced wife and her unruly progeny; she, in turn, despised Byron. Moreover, Byron's chief concern at the time was to look after the Gambas, whom the Tuscan government had ordered to leave the state by July 8. When Pietro Gamba and Count Gamba departed for Genoa — Teresa remained temporarily with her lover in Pisa — Byron was well aware that the real object of the persecution of the Gambas was to get him, the dangerous *"Signore Inglese,"* out of Italy.

In spite of the turbulent currents that eddied round him, Byron was once again enjoying the creative excitement of continuing his epic-satire, for Teresa had consented to the resumption of *Don Juan* — provided it be "more guarded and decorous and senti-mental" than before. Writing with relish and apparently ignoring the stipulations of his "Dictatress," Byron penned the hilariously erotic seraglio scene of Canto VI. But his underlying deep serious-ness does become manifest in the succeeding cantos of *Don Juan;* his Preface to Cantos VI, VII, and VIII is explicit in this regard, and Cantos VII and VIII contain his thoroughgoing satire of war.[11]

At midnight on July 12 two women with ghost-white faces arrived at the Casa Lanfranchi. Mary Shelley and Jane Williams had come by carriage from Lerici in search of Shelley and Wil-liams, who had sailed in their boat, *Ariel,* on July 8 from Leghorn for Lerici and had not been heard from since. An observer had seen the small boat disappear into the haze of a sudden squall off Via Reggio, and Trelawny had sent couriers along the coast; Byron and Hunt now joined him in the search. Not until July 18 was Shelley's body found on the beach at Via Reggio.

Byron was stunned by Shelley's death. Writing to Murray he said, "You were all brutally mistaken about Shelley, who was, without exception, the *best* and least selfish man I ever knew."[12] In response to Mary's desire that Shelley be buried in the Protestant Cemetery in Rome, Trelawny obtained permission from the Tuscan government for cremation of the remains. On August 16 Trelawny, Byron, and Hunt exhumed Shelley's body from the seashore and cremated it, throwing salt, incense, and wine on the fire which burned fiercely for three hours. The ashes were gathered into a lead box, inclosed in an oak coffin, and sealed for shipment to Rome.[13]

After Shelley's death, the relationship between Byron and Hunt deteriorated, although plans still went forward for the publication of the new literary journal, *The Liberal,* to which Byron had con-tributed *The Vision of Judgment;* moreover, Byron was proceeding rapidly with three new cantos of *Don Juan.* While Byron was pack-ing to leave with Teresa for Genoa, where Gamba and his son had found refuge after being expelled from Tuscany, Hobhouse arrived in Italy and visited Byron on September 15. Hobhouse found Byron much changed since their last meeting five years before in Venice, and he particularly noted Byron's burning interest in the Greek War of Independence.

Late in September Byron and Teresa left Pisa for Genoa in his coach, traveling by way of Lerici to take Mary Shelley with them.

Trelawny and the Hunts followed, and what remained of the Pisan Circle was resituated in Genoa. Byron and the Gambas were soon comfortably established in the palatial Casa Saluzzo on a hill overlooking Genoa and the bay. Byron lost no time in completing a tenth canto of *Don Juan* and beginning an eleventh.

On October 15 the first number of *The Liberal* was published in England by John Hunt, Leigh Hunt's brother; by the end of the month Byron had offered the latest cantos of *Don Juan* to John Hunt and withdrawn from Murray as publisher. *The Vision of Judgment,* published in the journal, was at once recognized as Byron's. The outcry against the poem was universal. It was vilified as wicked, impious, slanderous, and seditious; and John Hunt was prosecuted by The Constitutional Association for libel of George III. When Murray, with whom Byron continued to correspond was so tactless as to send Byron a copy of the *Quarterly Review* in which *Don Juan* was denounced as more wicked than *Cain,* Byron responded with a forthright declaration of his patently serious satirical purpose in his epic-satire: "*Don Juan* will be known by and bye, for what it is intended, — a *Satire* on *abuses* of the present states of Society..."[14]

CHAPTER 10

1823–1824 Byron in Greece:
Don Juan in Action

BYRON's increasing seriousness and restlessness at Genoa is evidenced by the themes and moods of his literary works in progress. In January he composed in heroic couplets *The Age of Bronze,* a savage satire; and by the end of March he had finished a fifteenth canto of *Don Juan;* carrying his Don through Russia and into England, Byron satirized war, despotism, and social hypocrisy. The only departure from his serious satire of this period was a brief reversion to his earlier popular manner, a romantic tale, *The Island,* based on Captain William Bligh's *Narrative of the Mutiny of the Bounty.*

I   Age of Bronze

Byron wrote *The Age of Bronze* in December, 1822, and in January, 1823, during a pause in the composition of *Don Juan.* It was published in April, 1823, by John Hunt, to whom Byron had changed as publisher. The poem was a return to the satiric manner and mode of the Augustan Age — a savage satire in heroic couplets directed chiefly against the Congress of Verona and war prosperity in England. The Allied Powers had met in Verona in November, 1822, to consider whether France should be permitted to invade Spain to crush the revolution that had broken out. Their decision to let France do as she pleased angered Byron, whose sympathies were with the insurgents in Spain. In his hard-hitting satire Byron denounced not only the Holy Alliance and Metternich but also international financiers, the "true war lords," and the domestic war profiteers — the English agriculturalists and manufacturers who prospered from the Napoleonic Wars and their aftermath on the

Continent. These Byron condemned as "The last to bid the cry of warfare cease, / The first to make a malady of peace." Here we have ample evidence of Byron's economic and social as well as political realism. The parallels offered by two world wars and their aftermaths in the twentieth century are conspicuous. It is unnecessary to point to the profitable war and post-war economy of our time and to the grave apprehension in financial circles over the recurring "threat of peace."

Byron now handled the heroic couplet with greater skill and effectiveness than in his earlier efforts, profiting by the versatility of his *ottava rima* versification. In a very brilliant *tour-de-force* of rhyme-repetition he rang the changes on "rent," his synonym for war profits (Sec. XIV). In this rhapsody of ridicule occur the words made famous by that other great Harrovian, Winston Churchill — "Blood, sweat, and tears."

> Safe in their barns these Sabine tillers sent
> Their brethren out to battle — why? for rent!
> They roared, they dined, they drank, they swore they meant   2
> To die for England — why then live? for rent!
> The peace had made one general malcontent
> Of these high-market patriots; war was rent!
> Their love of country, millions all mis-spent,
> How reconcile? by reconciling rent!
> And will they not repay the treasures lent?
> No: down with everything, and up with rent!
> Their good, ill, health, wealth, joy, or discontent,
> Being, end, aim, religion — *rent — rent — rent!*

In *The Age of Bronze,* regarded by one critic today as "not very good" and by another as "one of Byron's best satires," we see how Byron's satire has a truly modern ring as he derides international power politics and war prosperity, whether of the "hot" or "cold" war variety. Herein he gives further proof of his realistic awareness of the economic as well as social and political problems of a troubled era in all essential respects like our own. Whether a century ago or today, the shoe Byron cobbled fits!

II *Departure from Italy*

In April, 1823, Byron was visited by "the most gorgeous" Lady

Blessington and her husband, the Earl of Blessington.[1] This beautiful and brilliant woman, with her extraordinary understanding of men of literary and artistic ability, was deeply impressed by the perspicuity, candor, and charm of Byron which she later recorded in *Conversations of Lord Byron with the Countess of Blessington.* She perceptively discerned that Byron's frank censure of English society was owing to what Salvador de Madariaga has called Byron's "deep Englishry." She found that he detested English "cant" which he regarded as the enemy of "all that is pure and good" and which can be conquered only by exposing it to *"ridicule,* the only *weapon* . . . that the English climate cannot rust."[2]

Byron's complex and paradoxical nature Lady Blessington likewise observed. He said to her: "People take for gospel all I say, and go away continually with false impressions. *Mais n'importe!* it will render the statements of my future biographers more amusing. . . . Now, if I know myself, I should say, that I have no character at all. . . . I am so changeable, being everything by turns and nothing long, — I am such a strange *mélange* of good and evil, that it would be difficult to describe me. There are but two sentiments to which I am constant, — a strong love of liberty, and a detestation of cant. . ."[3]

The opportunity for which Byron was ripe came in April when Edward Blaquiere visited him on his way to Greece. As representative of the London Greek Committee formed to aid the Greeks in their War of Independence, Blaquiere sought Byron's advice and assistance. He was accompanied by Andreas Luriottis, representing the Greek provisional Government. Byron, gratified by the confidence reposed in him by the London Greek Committee and genuinely interested in the Greek cause, offered to go to Greece if he could be of any use to the Greek government. To this end he began at once to muster his financial resources to equip with medical and military supplies an expedition to Greece.

Byron was fully aware that the chief obstacle to his departure for Greece was Teresa. Both his affection for her and his desire for undivided commitment to the Greek cause were genuine, and he was torn. While he debated, he continued and finished a sixteenth canto of *Don Juan* and began a seventeenth; but he wrote only fourteen stanzas of it before he departed for Greece; in the words of Miss Boyd, "He completed *Don Juan* in action."[4] In May, Byron learned of his election to the London Greek Committee and of the Committee's gratitude and delight that he was willing to undertake the Greek adventure. But Byron still could not bring himself to pain Teresa by telling her of his resolve to leave for Greece.

The seriousness of Byron's "last attachment" to the woman whose redemptive and salutary influence had contributed so greatly to his most creative and productive literary period is shown in his genuine reluctance to separate from her.[5] He told Lady Blessington, "I am bound, by the indissoluble ties of marriage, to *one* who will *not* live with me, and live with one to whom I cannot give a legal right to be my companion. . . .Were the Contessa Guiccioli and I married, we should I am sure, be cited as an example of conjugal happiness . . ."[6]

Finally, he let Pietro, who was eager to accompany Byron to Greece, break the sad news to his sister: "To her a death-sentence would have seemed less terrible."[7] Anguished, she begged Byron to do the impossible — take her to Greece with him. Feeling depressed and guilty of neglecting Teresa, Byron tried lamely to make amends by giving her·a great bundle of his manuscripts, saying "Do what you like with them. . . .But perhaps some day they may be prized."[8] Byron had a fatalistic presentiment, which he did not disclose to Teresa, that he would die in Greece.

Spurred by a letter early in June from Blaquiere in Zante, Byron began purchasing medical supplies for the Greek cause from the six thousand pounds available from his own funds. His Genoese banker friend, Charles Barry, secured for Byron's expedition the *Hercules,* a one-hundred-and-twenty-ton English vessel. Trelawny, who was to accompany Byron on the Greek adventure, had the unpleasant task of making such alterations as were possible in the fittings of the clumsy "collier-built tub" of which he did not approve. Byron engaged as physician for the expedition Dr. Francesco Bruno, a young medic just out of the university. And Byron's romanticism led him to order for himself and for Pietro Gamba and Trelawny splendid uniforms in scarlet and gold, as well as three heroic helmets to be worn when they stepped on Greek shores.

Since the dangerous *"Signore Inglese"* was about to depart from Italy, Count Gamba was permitted to return to his home in Ravenna; and he wanted Teresa to go with him. Teresa realized the inevitability of her return but was anguished at the thought of separation from Byron. On July 13 Byron took his last, reluctant farewell of Teresa and went on board the *Hercules;* the next morning Teresa, with a heavy heart, began the carriage journey with her father to Ravenna. But the weather was not favorable until July 16 for departure from Genoa. Accompanied by Pietro, Trelawny, and Bruno, and taking with him ten thousand Spanish dollars, bills of exchange for forty thousand more, and medicines for a thousand men for a year, Byron sailed on the *Hercules* for Leghorn.[9]

At Leghorn a letter from the Greek patriot, Prince Constantine Mavrocordatos, urged Byron to ally himself with the Greek leader, Marco Botzaris, and advised him of the strategic importance of Missolonghi.[10] An early evidence of Byron's realism in the handling of the complex and often baffling practical aspects of his Greek adventure was his immediate decision to make Cephalonia his first destination and his eventual point of departure for Missolonghi on the Greek mainland. While he waited at Leghorn, Byron added a single-sentence postscript to Teresa to Pietro's letter to his sister: "...Believe that I always *love* you — and that a thousand words could only express the same idea. — ever dearest yours, N.B."[11] And he received a packet from Johann Wolfgang von Goethe containing verses by the illustrious German poet in praise of Byron.

On July 24 Byron sailed away from Leghorn. In Italy, as Marchand so discerningly says, "he had spent some of the happiest, and certainly the most productive, years of his life. He was being swept away toward Greece and an uncertain goal, partly by the inward compulsion of his own dissatisfaction, but more perhaps by the inevitable demand of circumstances and his own fame, which had combined with his weakness to drive him to do what was expected of him."[12] By the time the ship reached Argostoli, capital of Cephalonia, on August 3, Byron was in improved health and spirits (the effect the sea always had on him). Byron was cordially welcomed by Colonel Charles James Napier, the English Resident, a devoted Philhellene but nonetheless a judicious and astute critic of the dissension-torn Greeks. From Napier Byron first learned the facts of Greek disunity in the cause of independence and of contending rival factions.[13] He received this intelligence philosophically, resolving to wait in Cephalonia for sound directives from Captain Marco Botzaris and from Prince Alexander Mavrocordatos before proceeding to the mainland.

Meanwhile, Byron was delighted to meet again in Cephalonia some of the wild Suliote warriors whom he had admired in the

Epirus in 1809. He immediately hired a group of some fifty or more of these undisciplined but picturesque soldiers as a personal body-guard. While awaiting advice from the mainland, Byron decided to visit the adjacent island of Ithaca, reputedly the home of Homer's Odysseus. Byron enjoyed the experience, but the strenuous expedition demanded an open-boat crossing in broiling sun and prolonged riding and climbing over rough terrain. Twice during the five days Byron was briefly but severely ill. His apoplectic rage, triggered by the ceremonious welcome of the monks at the Santa Euphemia monastery above Samos, was probably owing to this illness.

Finally, Byron received enthusiastic word on August 22 from Marco Botzaris, the Suliote leader engaged in repelling the Turks in the mountains of Arcanania north of Missolonghi, who urged Byron to proceed without delay to Missolonghi. On the heels of this message came the dismal news of the death of Botzaris in battle. The other Greek leader on whom Byron was relying, Mavrocor-datos, Secretary of State of the Civil Party, was temporarily in hiding under the intimidation of Kolokotrones, leader of the Military Party. "It was only the healthy cynicism of Byron's view of human nature in general and the Greek character in particular," writes Marchand, "coupled with his longer view of the ultimate good of liberation of the land, that kept him from turning in disgust from the whole project."[14]

George Finlay, the eminent historian of Greece, also observed and commended Byron's political realism. "No stranger," he wrote, "estimated the character of the Greeks more correctly than Lord Byron."[15] When overtures from the several leaders of the Greek factions seeking Byron's financial aid poured in upon him, Byron judiciously remained uncommitted, awaiting the strategic time and place for his next move. "I did not come here to join a faction but a nation ..." he wrote in his journal.[16] He would wait for signs of unity in the Greek effort.

Throughout these trying circumstances Byron maintained an attitude of prudence, objectivity, and confidence, remaining stead-fastly loyal to "the Cause." Indeed, he was so involved that poetic composition, always Byron's habitual means of expressing his strongest drives and deepest feelings, no longer occupied his time. "Poetry," he told Pietro, "should only occupy the idle."[17] Apparently, he never continued the fragment of the seventeenth canto, begun in Genoa, of *Don Juan.* At home in England, though Byron did not know it, John Hunt had published Cantos VI, VII, and VIII in July; and, before the end of 1823, he was to publish Cantos IX to XIV.

Early in September, the restless Trelawny departed for the seat of the Greek provisional government in the Morea; and Byron, with Pietro and Bruno, settled down in a small house at Metaxata to await developments. Meanwhile, Byron carried on a shrewd and sensible correspondence with the London Committee regarding the uncertainties and necessities of the Greek effort. Among the problems about which the committee sought his advice was the question of the wisdom of an English loan to the Greek government. In the meantime, Byron decided to make a personal loan to the Greek fleet to bring them out of hiding at Hydra and encourage them to engage the Turkish blockade of Missolonghi. To this end, he signed a contract on November 13 for a loan of four thousand pounds.

About this time, Colonel Leicester Stanhope, representing the London Greek Committee, arrived at Cephalonia, an impractical exponent of Jeremy Bentham's utilitarianism and quite the opposite of the realistic Colonel Napier. Stanhope believed that it would be necessary only to set up printing presses and to propagate republican principles in order to accomplish the deliverance of the Greeks. Byron's political realism is nowhere better revealed than in his letter at this time to the executive and legislative branches of the Greek government in the Morea introducing Colonel Stanhope:

...I must frankly confess, that unless union and order are established, all hopes of a loan will be in vain; and all the assistance which the Greeks could expect from abroad ... will be suspended or destroyed. ... I desire the well-being of Greece, and nothing else; I will do all I can to secure it; but I cannot consent ... that the English public ... should be deceived as to the real state of Greek affairs. The rest, gentlemen, depends on you: you have fought gloriously; act honorably towards your fellow-citizens and towards the world ...[18]

Greek affairs took a turn for the worse in December when civil war broke out between the executive and legislative branches of the government in the Morea. And, although during the entire period of Byron's eventual stay at Missolonghi the governmental efforts were stalemated by factional strife, "...Byron's part in getting the deputies started for England, as well as his efforts to get the loan launched and his aid to the fleet and to Mavrocordatos," writes Marchand, "did. in the long run have a far-reaching effect on the progress of the Revolution. Certainly he judged rightly in not going to Eastern Greece in 1823. He would only have lost the personal prestige which eventually made his name a unifying force in Greece."[19]

III   *Byron at Missolonghi*

From Mavrocordatos, who had landed at Missolonghi on December 11, came to Byron an enthusiastic letter urging him to come at once to Missolonghi and saying that he was sending a ship to convey Byron there. "On reaching Missolonghi," Mavrocordatos wrote, "I found moreover that everyone was so convinced of the truth of what I now tell you, that you will be received here as a saviour. Be assured, My Lord, that it depends only on yourself to secure the destiny of Greece..."[20] As a result of this letter, Byron hired two island boats and put Pietro Gamba in charge of the larger one, a "bombard," to transport the horses and supplies. Taking on board with him Dr. Bruno, Fletcher, and Loukas Chalandritsanos, a handsome youth of sixteen whose family Byron had befriended, he set sail in his fast "mistico" on December 30, 1823, for Missolonghi.

The journey to Missolonghi was not uneventful. The two boats became separated and experienced a series of mishaps and narrow escapes from Turkish vessels. Pietro reached Missolonghi on January 4 and Byron on the evening of the same day. Donning his military uniform, Byron landed the next morning amid the firing of salutes from each ship of the Greek squadron in the harbor and the welcoming shouts of soldiery and citizenry. As Byron approached the house where Prince Mavrocordatos and a retinue of Greek officers awaited him, the guns of the fort fired a salvo of twenty-one guns.

Mavrocordatos disclosed to Byron his plans for the capture of Lepanto, the only Turkish stronghold on the north side of the Gulf of Corinth. This victory accomplished, the taking of Patras on the south shore of the Gulf could be more readily effected. With Corinth and Patras achieved, the Greeks would control the entire Gulf and could hope to unite Arcarnania and Aetolia with the

Morea. Mavrocordatos' suggestion that the English lord lead the attack on Lepanto appealed to Byron's romantic nature and intrepid spirit. Now it seemed to him that both the time and the situation were favorable to his accomplishing some concrete action for "the Cause." He was not dismayed or discouraged by the swampy, cheerless town of Missolonghi with its ill-favored setting on a marshy promontory jutting into the shallow lagoon, or the uncomfortable house at the end of the promontory, or the cold, rainy weather. He had cast his lot with the people and country he loved, and there was no turning back.

The four or five thousand soldiers who had followed Mavrocordatos from all parts of Greece, the five hundred Suliotes whom Byron agreed to support and train as a corps, and the citizenry of Missolonghi — all hailed Byron as a hero. Both the executive and legislative branches of the Greek government sent messages to Byron as the benefactor of Greece, expressing their appreciation and their hope that he would use his influence to secure the launching of the English loan.

On the evening of his thirty-sixth birthday, something prompted Byron to take a long look at the bright dreams of his youth, his fevered life, and the elusive ambitions of the present. The next morning, January 22, 1824, Byron wrote in his journal the ten stanzas of "On This Day I Complete my Thirty-Sixth Year," — one of the last poems he ever penned.

. . . .
My days are in the yellow leaf;
    The flowers and fruits of love are gone;
The worm, the canker, and the grief
    Are mine alone!
. . . .
The Sword, the Banner, and the Field,
    Glory and Greece, around me see!
The Spartan, borne upon his shield,
    Was not more free.
. . . .
If thou regret'st thy youth, why live?
    The land of honourable death
Is here: — up to the Field, and give
    Away thy breath!

· ·
> Seek out — less often sought than found —
> A soldier's grave, for thee the best;
> Then look around, and choose thy ground,
> And take thy Rest.

Byron soon realized that Mavrocordatos and the Greeks were expecting him to shoulder the entire responsibility for financing and leading the three thousand troops against Lepanto. William Parry, the English firemaster sent by the London Committee with equipment and technicians for an artillery brigade, arrived at Missolonghi on February 5. The practical-minded Parry realistically sized up the harassments and discouragements of Byron at Missolonghi. Byron, he concluded, had no friends in Greece he could trust and no personal comfort nor security: Mavrocordatos was well-meaning but indecisive; the Suliotes were ungovernable, deceitful, and greedy for Byron's dollars. Although the poet laughed outwardly at his difficulties, "in his heart, he felt that he was forlorn and forsaken."[21]

But Byron's disillusionment reached its peak in mid-February when, taking stock of the number of Suliote troops that could be mustered for the attack on Lepanto, he discovered that the Suliote chieftains had padded the rolls with non-existent soldiers. Byron burst into a violent rage and declared that he would have nothing further to do with the irresponsible Suliotes: "They may go to the Turks, or the Devil. . . . For the rest, I hold my means and person at the disposal of the Greek nation and Government the same as before."[22]

Byron was dispirited as he saw the planned attack on Lepanto vaporizing before his eyes. The assault must of necessity be postponed because of inadequate forces. On the evening of February 15 Byron suffered a severe seizure, possibly apoplectic, which nearly took his life. His condition was aggravated by a bungling effort to bleed him on the part of Bruno and Millingen, a young English medical volunteer. Endless annoyances and tragic mishaps followed one upon another in Missolonghi in late February as Byron recovered slowly from his serious illness. To Pietro Gamba he confided: "I begin to fear that I have done nothing but lose time, money, patience, and health; but I was prepared for it. . . . I ought to make up my mind to meet with deception, and calumny, and ingratitude."[23] Nevertheless, with unflagging courage, despite constant reverses and deteriorating health, Byron continued to pour his fortune and energy into the uncertain Greek cause.

Toward the end of February Byron was both pleased and embarrassed to learn from Hobhouse and Kinnaird that he was now regarded in England as a hero because of his Greek adventure. At the same time, he was encouraged by the news of John Hunt's success with the new cantos of *Don Juan*. When George Finlay arrived from Athens bringing an invitation to Byron and Mavrocordatos from the strongest leader of Eastern Greece, Odysseus, to meet at Salona for a congress of all Greek factions with the purpose of achieving unity and making common cause against the Turks, Byron and Mavrocordatos decided to go to do so in mid-March.

As March advanced, Byron insisted on keeping up his riding in the chilly, rainy weather, in spite of his precarious health and recurring vertigo and nervous tension. On March 17 he wrote his last letter to Teresa, an affectionate but unrealistic one that shared none of his hopes and fears, and that could not have brought comfort to the lonely young woman in Italy.

The Greek government in the Morea now urged him to come to Kranidi and to accept the post of governor-general of Greece. Byron politely declined the invitation, saying that he must first go to the congress at Salona, after which he would be at the government's service.[24] As March drew to a close, the weather grew steadily worse, and by March 27 when Byron had hoped to leave for Salona the roads were impassable and the rivers unfordable.

Byron's spirits were now at their lowest ebb and not without reason: his dream of leading the Suliotes to capture Lepanto had failed, and his chief and most ambitious hope of uniting the warring Greek factions now seemed to him illusory. Circumstances had prevented his attending the congress at Salona, and the Greek fleet had again dispersed. Trelawny and Stanhope, he felt, had deserted him; the Greek Committee in London he mistakenly supposed were indifferent or disapproving. Byron felt, Sir Harold Nicolson concludes, that he had lost his health, reputation, and honor.[25] He felt that only one thing remained for him to do: "For by then Byron had realised that the only thing he could do for Greece was not to run away."[26] "He knew that the only positive action of which he was still capable was death."[27]

IV *Illness and Death*

In April Byron's health rapidly deteriorated as he experienced irritability, frequent vertigo, and general debility of body and mind; but he made every effort to regain his characteristic composure and resolute manner. He was deeply moved on April 9 by a letter of gratitude and commendation from his oldest and best friend, Hobhouse, who wrote: "Nothing can be more serviceable to the cause than all you have done — Everybody is more than pleased and content — As for myself, I only trust that the great sacrifices which you have made may contribute ... to the final success of the great cause — This will indeed be doing something worth living for — and will make your name and character stand far above those of any contemporary."[28]

On the same day Byron was caught in a heavy rain on returning from riding. In the evening he suffered fever and severe rheumatic pains, but he still insisted on riding out again the next morning. By April 12 Byron was severely ill, and Parry obtained his reluctant consent to take him by boat to Zante for medical care; but a sirocco, followed by hurricane winds, made it impossible for any vessel to set sail. Byron's doctors, Bruno and Millingen, now began their persistent and prolonged insistence on bleeding which Byron adamantly refused. Distrustful of the competence of his doctors, alarmingly ill, and frequently delirious, Byron found some comfort only in the presence of Parry, who visited him often and acted as a buffer against the doctors who daily demanded bleeding. Parry was moved to great pity for the younger man, who was the helpless victim of confusion, inefficiency, and want of understanding care. "There was the gifted Lord Byron," Parry wrote, "who had been the object of universal attention ... intoxicated with the idolatry of men, and the more flattering love of women, gradually expiring, almost forsaken, and certainly without the consolation ... of breathing out his last sigh in the arms of some dear friend."[29]

Finally, on April 16, threatened by the doctors with the possibility of loss of his reason if bleeding were not allowed, Byron yielded angrily to their importunities, "Come, you are, I see, a damn'd set of butchers. Take away as much blood as you will; but have done with it."[30] As their patient weakened and his resistance decreased, the doctors continued taking his blood. He became more tranquil;

but, as Marchand says, "It was the tranquility of a man whose vital forces had been drained."[31]

By Easter Sunday, Bruno, seeing in Byron signs of approaching death, insisted upon more bleeding. Later in the day, when Byron realized that his death was imminent, he said to Millingen: "Your efforts to preserve my life will be in vain. Die I must: I feel it. Its loss I do not lament; for to terminate my wearisome existence I came to Greece. — My wealth, my abilities, I devoted to her cause. — Well: there is my life to her."[32] Among his last utterances was a sentence in Italian: *"Io lascio qualche cosa di caro nel mondo; per il resto son contento di morire."* The Marchesa Origo translates this as "I leave something dear in the world; as to the rest, I am glad to die." And she implies that he meant *someone,* who might well have been Teresa.[33] It is equally possible, as Marchand suggests, that *something* meant his unfinished efforts in behalf of the liberation of Greece.[34]

He tried to convey his last words to his faithful Fletcher, but after chiefly incoherent efforts in which he repeatedly murmured the names of his wife, his child, his sister, and Hobhouse, he realized that Fletcher had not understood him, and that it was too late to try again. About six o'clock on the evening of Easter Sunday he murmured his last words; "I want to sleep now." He turned on his back and shut his eyes. Marchand writes, "The doctors now had him in their power, and they applied leeches to his temples. The blood flowed from his already impoverished veins all night."[35]

While he lay in this comatose state, letters arrived from Hobhouse and Kinnaird in England with cheering news of the achievement of the Greek loan, Mr. Canning's approval of "the Cause," and the London Committee's resolution of high praise and gratitude for Byron's exertions in the cause of Greek Independence. But the gratitude and praise came too late for Lord Byron to be aware of it. At six o'clock on the evening of April 19, 1824, during a terrific electrical storm, Byron opened his eyes once more and then closed them forever.

Byron's death at Missolonghi accomplished more for Greek unity and liberty than all his utterances and actions. Mavrocordatos, in behalf of the Provisional Government of Western Greece, proclaimed general Greek mourning. Funeral services for Byron were held in the Missolonghi church on April 22; but, as the tragic news traveled throughout Greece, every town and village held its own memorial service for "the great man." The Executive Branch in Nauplia proclaimed that, "because Byron does not walk any more on the Greek land, which he had loved so much years ago, and because Greece is grateful to him forever, and the Nation must give him the name of a father and benefactor . . . it is ordered that the 5th of May be regarded as a day of mourning. . ."[36] From that day Byron became a national hero of Greece and almost a legend. Songs, odes, and klephtic ballads were composed about him, such as the following one sung among the soldiers:

> Missolonghi groaned and the Suliots cried   5
> For Lord Byron who came from London. . . .
> The Klephts gave to Byron the name of father
> Because he loved the klephts of Roumele. . . .
> The woodlands weep, and the trees weep . . .
> Because Byron lies dead at Missolonghi.[37]

Greece has never forgotten Byron. From Attica to the farthest reaches of the Peloponnesus, Epirus, and Thessaly, Byron statues and memorials abound; and nearly every town has its "Odos Byronos" or Byron Street. In Athens a magnificent sculpture-group standing outside the Zappion at the juncture of two principal avenues depicts Hellas crowning Lord Byron with immortal laurels. Whenever the name of Lord Byron is mentioned, the eyes of the modern Greek brighten, and his tone is reverential as he murmurs, "Lordos Viron."

Byron's doctors had the unpleasant task of performing an autopsy and embalming the body for shipment to England. The perfect symmetry of the body was marred only by the club foot, but the cranium was like that of an octogenarian. A modern diagnosis of the cause of death, based on examination of all the evidence, is uremic poisoning aggravated by numerous bleedings and purgings.[38] On May 2 Byron's body left Missolonghi amid military honors enroute for Zante. From thence, the body departed May 24 on board the *Florida* for England where it finally arrived June 29, accompanied by Byron's most devoted follower, Pietro Gamba, whose sister Teresa received the heart-breaking news "with grief, but dignity."[39] And, when word of Byron's death reached England by express on May 14, Hobhouse and Kinnaird were desolated, Augusta was overwhelmed, and Lady Byron was deeply distressed.

London was thunderstruck, and the gloom of Byron's passing spread like a pall over Europe.

Byron's closest friends, zealous to protect his reputation from his own self-disclosures, bethought themselves of his "Memoirs" that had been given to Moore and deposited with Murray. Hobhouse, Kinnaird, and Murray favored their destruction; Moore, the only one of the men who had read the manuscript, was opposed. On May 17, in the spacious parlor of Murray's publishing house, Byron's friends, Hobhouse, Kinnaird, Murray, and Moore, gathered with Horton, Augusta's representative, and with Doyle, Lady Byron's agent. After heated debate, and in spite of Moore's remonstrances, Horton and Doyle tore up the manuscript and put it in the fireplace.[40]

When Byron's body arrived in England, Hobhouse met the ship and saw the remains of his best friend conveyed to a house in Great George Street. While the body lay in state on July 9 and 10, the Dean of Westminster refused burial in the Abbey. Byron's greatest biographer, Professor Leslie A. Marchand, has remarked in a tone most appropriately Byronic, "So far the Abbey has been unsullied by any reminder that Byron ever lived. Recently, however, a plaque was unveiled there to the memory of Keats and Shelley. Perhaps another hundred years will wash Byron's memory as white as that of Charles II."[41] Finally, on May 8, 1969, at the instigation of The Poetry Society of Great Britain, a white marble floor memorial to Lord Byron was unveiled by Mr. William Plomer, President of the Poetry Society, a laurel wreath was placed by C. Day Lewis, England's then Poet Laureate, and Dr. Abbott, Dean of Westminster Abbey, pronounced a benediction. So a century and a half of disapproval and neglect came to an end as the name of Lord Byron was entered among those of his peers in Poet's Corner of Westminster Abbey.

On July 12 Byron's funeral cortege passed from Great George Street, through Oxford Street, along Tottenham Court Road, and out of London by Highgate hill enroute to Nottingham. The hearse was followed by two coaches carrying his closest friends and by a large number of empty carriages sent out of deference by the great families who wished to abstain from any other participation. Throngs of people filled the streets to witness the solemn pomp as the procession of forty-seven carriages passed by. Four days later,

at the final rites in little Hucknall Church near Newstead, Hobhouse was struck by the extreme contrast between the "gorgeous
apparel of the coffin and urn and the coronet and the appearance
of the humble church."[42]

On Friday, July 16, Lord Byron was laid to rest in the tomb of
his ancestors beneath the chancel of Hucknall Torkard Church near
Newstead Abbey. Mourned by the Greeks as a national hero and
regarded throughout Europe as "the Trumpet Voice of Liberty,"
Byron's own prophetic words in *Childe Harold* best express the
essence of "The Pilgrim of Eternity":

> But I have lived, and have not lived in vain:
> My mind may lose its force, my blood its fire,
> And my frame perish even in conquering pain;
> But there is that within me which shall tire
> Torture and Time, and breathe when I expire ...   4

CHAPTER 11

1818–1824 Don Juan:
Epic Satire

A S already noted, John Hookham Frere's mock-heroic poem, *The Monks and the Giants,* written under the pen-name of "the brothers Whistlecraft," came to Byron's attention in September, 1817, and supplied him with what he called his "immediate *model*" for *Beppo* and *Don Juan. Whistlecraft,* written in imitation of Pulci's *Morgante Maggiore,* was Byron's introduction to the style and manner of Italian "burlesque" poetry in *ottava rima.* There is no evidence that Byron had in 1817 any firsthand acquaintance with the works of Pulci or Berni, but he had enjoyed Casti's *Animali Parlanti* and *Novelle Galanti.* Encouraged by Jeffrey's praise in the *Edinburgh Review* of *Beppo* (published in February, 1818), Byron read William Stewart Rose's free translation of Casti's *Animali Parlanti* and began investigating the Italian writers of mock-heroic verse, regarding them as the real precursors of the style he had adopted from Frere. In the spring of 1818 Byron wrote Murray, "If *Beppo* pleases, you shall have more in a year or two in the same mood."[1] And, as we have seen, he had already begun *Don Juan* when, on July 10, he wrote Murray that he had "two Stories, one serious and one ludicrous (*a la Beppo*), not yet finished, and in no hurry to be so."[2] After originally and mistakenly crediting Berni with being the "originator" of the Italian "burlesque" style, Byron later undertook his own translation of Pulci's *Morgante Maggiore,* and acknowledged in *Don Juan* (IV, vi) that "Pulci was sire of the half-serious rhyme."

I *Models*

Clearly, Byron was firmly resolved in the spring of 1818 to

139

undertake a great poem — a major work. Urged on by Gifford, Murray, and Shelley to "some greater enterprise of thought," he determined that it must be an epic, but one with a difference — a realistic epic, true to life and with an ordinary man as hero. For models he would begin with the Classic epic writers, Homer and Virgil, move on to Ariosto and Tasso, and draw especially upon the Italian jocose epic writers, Pulci, Berni, and Casti. To these he would add the example of the masters of satiric prose romance: Rabelais, Cervantes, Le Sage, Swift, Voltaire, Fielding, Smollett, and Sterne. And the "real model of *Don Juan,*" as Miss Boyd correctly observes, "is the picaresque novel, the great catchall of narrative and reflection, subject to no law but the author's desires."[3] Fielding, especially, furnished Byron with models for *Don Juan,* in epic intention, in the character of the protagonist, in the showman-narrator technique, in purposeful digression, and in urbanity of style.[4]

This is not to say, as Calvert reminds us, that Byron neglected the earlier models of the epic. In fact, he had them constantly in mind, experimenting with their methods and techniques, adapting them creatively to his fresh approach, and shaping and stamping the whole with his personality.[5] "My poem's epic," Byron declares and means it, in what Calvert calls his "real preface" (Canto I, 200–7). Playfully, he enumerates the correspondence of his poem with the traditional paraphernalia and conventions of the epic, "with strict regard to Aristotle's rules," but, actually, he is indulging in good-natured raillery against the neo-Classic Rules in order to assert his creative independence of them. He is adapting the past to the present, writing a modern epic that cannot be judged by the inherited Rules.[6] "His classical spirit is more subconscious than conscious..."[7] Byron knew what he wanted to do and set about doing it — in his own way.[8]

Much closer and more congenial to his intention and mood than the Ancients were the Renaissance epic writers, Ariosto and Tasso. From Ariosto he may have learned quite early the potentialities of the "medley" style, providing him with the basic devices which he refined and exploited; whimsical digression; plunges from pathos to bathos; colloquialism; and the serio-comic use of *ottava rima.*[9] But it was from Pulci, who first combined digression and colloquialism with high subjects, as well as from Berni and Casti, that Byron learned the most. His indebtedness to Pulci is clearly delineated by R. D. Waller in the introduction to his edition of Frere's *The Monks and the Giants* which provides, also, a succinct survey of *ottava rima* and the Pulcian imitations in English.[10]

The full range and importance of Byron's indebtedness in *Don Juan* to the general tradition of the eighteenth-century English novel has been thoroughly treated by Andras Horn in a monograph on this subject.[11] Byron profoundly admired Fielding whom he called the "*prose* Homer" and whose *Joseph Andrews,* Fielding's "comic epic in prose," he may have thought of as a model for his own poetic mock-epic in a realistic contemporary setting, as I have suggested elsewhere.[12] Likewise, from Sterne he learned the technique of purposeful digression; the rapid alternation from grave to gay, sentiment to satire; the management of tone and sentence structure; and the ingratiating combination of naughtiness, wisdom, and high comedy. Like Sterne, Byron could, in Miss Boyd's inimitable phrase, "float a shred of story in an ocean of rambling reflection and metaphysical speculation."[13]

In sum, Byron had in mind as models the Classic epic, Italian comic epic, satiric prose romance, and picaresque novel when he began *Don Juan.*

II   *Materials*

Byron's answer to Murray's question about his "plan" for *Don Juan* was not merely facetious: "I *have* no plan — I *had* no plan; but I had or have materials."[14] Byron *did* have a plan, an open-ended one, that would allow him personal and artistic freedom to roam without restraint as his epic conception expanded and developed. And he *did* have materials, abundant materials: incidents and ideas from his wide and retentive reading; and "*real* life" from his own remarkably wide and diversified personal experience. Literature and life, skillfully fused, contribute simultaneously to all Byron's best poetry; and *Don Juan* is the shining example. *Don Juan* is indeed a compound of literary reminiscence and self-expression. This combination is made abundantly clear by Miss Boyd in her definitive account of Byron's reading and her thorough analysis of the broad and diversified range of his materials and his discriminating use of them to develop the kaleidoscopic changes in scene and temper of his modern epic.[15]

Byron's epigraph for *Don Juan,* selected from Horace's *Ars*

Poetica, "Difficile est proprie communia dicere" (It is hard to treat in your own way what is common), is most appropriate; for Byron was trying to treat freshly familiar literary subjects and "common life." Especially was it appropriate for what appeared to be a new version of the Don Juan legend.[16] Actually, as Joseph suggests, Byron was not interested in retelling the Don Juan story but in reconstructing it afresh on the level of high comedy.

Wanting a hero, and finding that the modern age does not provide a "true one," Byron says, resignedly, "I'll therefore take our ancient friend Don Juan — / We all have seen him, in the pantomime, / Sent to the Devil somewhat ere his time." Byron undoubtedly was acquainted with the familiar theatrical treatments of the Don Juan legend, from its initial dramatic appearance in Tirso de Molina's El Burlador de Sevilla in the seventeenth century, through Molière's Le Festin de Pierre, to the Don Giovanni of Mozart and Da Ponte which he must have seen at Venice, as well as Goldoni's comedy, Il Dissoluto, based on Molière. And he had frequently seen in London the Garrick-Delpini pantomime based on Thomas Shadwell's Libertine.[17]

But more relevant than any of these dramatic treatments of the legend was Byron's reading of Coleridge's critique of Shadwell's Libertine in Biographia Literaria, Chapter XXIII. Helene Richter believes that Byron owed his new conception of Don Juan to Coleridge's delineation of him. Coleridge describes him, writes Miss Boyd, "as the natural man, to whom the only sin is to act contrary to his nature." This description, Miss Boyd observes, tallies very closely with the public image of Byron in England in 1816. The similarity may very well have commended the legend to the egocentric Byron's attention as promising material for his epic purposes, but he saw fit to alter and adapt it freely to his own view of human life.[18]

Byron's Don Juan is almost the antithesis of the legendary Don, who is libertine, a heartless seducer, and a ruthless monster who deserves his supernatural punishment. But Byron's hero is a "very broth of a boy," good-hearted, chivalrous, well-meaning, "more sinned against than sinning," who, like Candide or Tom Jones, survives harrowing adventures and gains a degree of wisdom from his experiences. Juan and Tom are much alike in their instinctive courage and innate goodness, qualities which bring them through severe trials with manly fortitude and increased discretion. Ronald

Bottrall rightly defines the essential nature of these kindred heroes. Both are natural men who act from healthy impulse, not from social convention. They are in sharp contrast with the evil in society, fundamental hypocrisy and unconcern for individual humanity. In both Juan and Tom, the evil, if it be evil, is "mainly sexual; or at worst, anything vaguely against the social usage."[19] Byron's Juan, then, has virtually nothing in common with the diabolical Don of the myth.

Miss Richter, remarking the kinship of the two great Renaissance folk heroes, Don Juan and Faust, asserts that Byron treated the Juan-saga symbolically as the companion piece to the Faust-saga.[20] Joseph suggests that Byron may have had a more subtle parallel in mind. Both myths treat of the natural man who knows no law but appetite: in Faust, the appetite is for power and knowledge; in Don Juan, for the fulfillment of sense and passion. Byron's *Manfred* and other "theological" dramas are indebted to the Faust myth through Goethe's masterpiece. Byron in his *Don Juan* may have had in mind the natural man, emancipated from compulsive libertinism, as "enlightened rationalist" and "intellectual chameleon," moving with free-lance ease through the modern world.[21]

In the light of Byron's scant use of the character and adventures of the legendary Don, Miss Boyd very appropriately raises the question as to whether Byron owes anything of consequence to the Don Juan legend. Suffice it to say, with Joseph (p. 208), that Byron reconstituted the myth in a form congruent with his age and his own experience. Portraying society on the verge of revolution and war, he is able to achieve a wide-ranging contemporaneousness, an applicability to the 1790 period, the time-framework of the poem, as well as to his own age, the post-Napoleonic Wars era. And, I may add, the contemporaneity of his satiric portrait is almost equally valid for the two post-world war eras of the twentieth century.[22]

Another source mentioned by Byron, in addition to the Spanish legend, is the real-life story of "Anacharsis" Cloots, a French émigré, cosmopolite, apostle of liberty, and man of letters, who was executed in 1794 during the Reign of Terror. Byron was attracted to Jean Baptiste "Anacharsis" Cloots as a highly congenial spirit and conspicuous Philhellenist who had rejected his Christian name in favor of that of the celebrated philosophical traveler in Ancient Greece. The time-framework of *Don Juan* could well have been suggested by the career of Anacharsis Cloots, the few years of the spirited Cloots' adventures being comparable with the young Juan's from 1789 to 1791. Byron hinted that he might have Juan end in the French Revolution, or in Hell, or in an unhappy marriage, not knowing which would be the worst. As Miss Boyd observes, Byron's superimposing of the actual story of Cloots in the French Revolution upon the career of the legendary Don shows the strong preference of the fact-loving Byron for real and authentic materials.[23]

For his wide-ranging spectrum of incidents, Byron draws upon the common domain of traditional tales, fabliaux, popular ballads, and romances, as was the wont of Shakespeare, Chaucer, and Boccaccio; and Miss Boyd's account of this is full and definitive.[24] Byron freely intermingles literary incidents with his own personal experiences as in the Julia episode of Canto I. The situation is a commonplace in popular literature; analogues of the familiar plot — the amours of a young wife and her lover are betrayed by a lost article of clothing — abound in fabliaux and comedy from Apuleius and Boccaccio to Casti's *Novelle Amorose*. Casti's fourth *novella, La Diavolessa,* provides a close analogue of Juan's adventures in Cantos I and II.

Voyage and shipwreck details like those in Canto II have been conventional features of the epic since the *Odyssey*. Supremely celebrated by Daniel Defoe in *Robinson Crusoe,* shipwrecks have been vividly detailed from Ariosto's *Orlando Furioso* to Tobias Smollett's sea novels. Byron drew not only on John Dunlop's *History of Fiction,* but especially on George Dalzell's *Shipwrecks and Disasters at Sea* (1812) for a prose documentation of Juan's shipwreck. And for poetic authority he had William Falconer's *Shipwreck* (1762), a favorite of Byron's, recounting man's losing struggle with the sea. Byron excels Falconer by virtue of his "hard-boiled" manner, lowered emotional tone, and prosaic realism. All of this information Byron corroborated and augmented by painstaking research and by his own close call in 1809 in attempting to sail from Prevesa to Patras in a Turkish ship.

The pattern of shipwreck, rescue by a lovely maiden, natural and passionate young love, and piracy in the Mediterranean is as old as the Greek romances, all of which were recounted in Dunlop's *History of Fiction*. Many of these, such as *Daphnis and Chloe,* were in Byron's Venetian library. He may not have known their medieval equivalents, *Floires and Blanceflor* and *Aucassin and Nicolette;* but he knew their modern counterparts, *Paul and Virginie* and Christoph Martin Wieland's *Oberon.* Daphnis and Chloe, however, as Miss Boyd reminds us, are the true literary ancestors of Juan and Haidée, whose idyllic love unfortunately does not end happily as in the Greek romance. On Wieland's *Oberon* Byron relied for the scene in Canto V between Juan and the imperious and voluptuous harem queen Gulbeyaz. Byron far surpasses Wieland in psychological penetration of his characters and in narrative realism.

Byron's obsessive desire to achieve exact verisimilitude led him to the Marquis de Castelnau's *Histoire de la Nouvelle Russie* (1820) for the authentic details of the Siege of Ismail in Canto VI. Thomas Hope's novel, *Anastasius* (1819), Byron admired and envied, and he may well have followed its suggestions for the later narrative pattern of *Don Juan.* The enterprising Anastasius has many adventures that parallel Juan's, such as moving from Constantinople to St. Petersburg and becoming a lover of the Empress Catherine. And both heroes experience parallel situations in visiting strange lands and engaging in similar ironic reflections on foreign customs and conventions.[25]

Byron's indebtedness to literature goes beyond incidents to ideas, as Miss Boyd amply demonstrates. Most notable is the example of Byron's satiric view of war which pervades Cantos VII, VIII, and IX of *Don Juan.* His despite for the inhumanity and futility of war goes back to Lucian and Juvenal, to the preface of Robert Burton's *Anatomy of Melancholy* with its comprehensive denunciation of wars of conquest as the major crime of civilization, to Pope's *Essay on Man,* to Johnson's *Vanity of Human Wishes,* and to Fielding's *Miscellanies* and *Jonathan Wild.* Ideas from all these were prominently in Byron's thoughts in 1821, and he made vigorous application of them to modern life when he resumed *Don Juan* in 1822. Likewise, he probably knew Benjamin Constant's pamphlet, *Esprit de Conquête et de l'Usurpation* (1813), the most celebrated anti-militaristic statement of Byron's day with its emphasis on the hypocrisy and economic futility of war in the modern world, so remarkably prophetic of our own time. And Byron used Castelnau's *Histoire,* mentioned above, not only for incidents but as a point of departure for antithetically different ideas about war. Castelnau glorifies war as heroic, but Byron launches the major attack of his epic satire against war as the nadir of unnatural civilization.[26]

In the English cantos of *Don Juan,* the last six, less literary influence appears, but there are correspondences, Miss Boyd notes, from biography, memoirs, and novels. The Count de Grammont's memoirs show Byron how to capture the essential spirit of a social period, contemporary periodicals provide a rich source of allusions and digressions, and Fanny Burney's novels of social manners were well known to Byron. In his description of Norman Abbey, Byron burlesques the Gothic novel treatment of haunted country houses, especially in the ghost scenes of Canto XVI where Byron's skeptical humor and realism delights in the natural explanation of the supernatural. And the latter cantos of *Don Juan* reflect both the techniques and opinions of Thomas Love Peacock's satirical novel *Melincourt* (1817) with its realistic pictures of English high society which closely parallel Byron's in the English cantos. For the quality of "tough reasonableness" which Byron learned from his fellow satirist, Joseph aptly coins the term "Peacockian."[27]

And, finally, Byron draws his materials for *Don Juan* not only from a host of literary incidents and materials but, as we have noted, from his own broad and diversified personal experience. We must agree with Calvert that *"Don Juan* is drawn from real life, either that of the author or of people he knew...."[28] Especially is this true of the English cantos where Byron is describing the social milieu he knew intimately. Notable examples are the matter-of-factness of Byron's vivid pictures of sea voyages and of the sea itself, for which he had such affinity; the Levant scenes he had known in his early *Childe Harold* wanderings; and the London *haut ton* of Byron's years of fame, 1812–1816.

For both the male and female characters of *Don Juan* Byron could draw on a broad spectrum of personal experience virtually without rival in his day. "What a gallery of figures!" exclaims Miss Boyd: hypocritical Donna Inez; Haidée, "the caressed one"; her "piratical papa," Lambro; Gulbeyaz, the voluptuous harem queen; Dudu, Lolah, and Katinka, the beauteous odalisques (probably from the Macri sisters at Athens); Johnson, soldier of fortune; bloody Suvaroff; Catherine, "queen of sovereigns and whores"; Lady Adeline, acme of sophistication; Aurora Raby, ingenuous and gemlike; and an almost endless number of others. And back of all these were real men and women the poet had known. Even the time-framework of the narrative, from 1789 to 1791, is paralleled by a second framework, that of the narrator, thirty years later, the post-Napoleonic era.

Using Scott's Waverly novels as a model of picaresque narrative in which the protagonist's adventures involve both fictitious characters and historical events, Byron produced a typically Byronic "medley." Upon a very minimum of the elements of the Don Juan legend, he superimposed the historical pattern of an actual figure of the French Revolution; and, modeling his "epic" after the classic epic, Italian comic epic, and Fielding's "comic epic in prose," he achieved at once a novel in verse and an epic satire of modern Europe.[29] "Byron," writes Jerome McGann, "of the poets of his age who wrote epic poems, was the only one who completely solved the problem of epic style for a modern poem."[30]

III *Composition and Growth*

Murray and his literary advisors in London, as well as Walter Scott, were delighted with *Beppo;* and Murray urged Byron to send him another lively tale in the same vein. Encouraged by the reception of the experimental poem in his new Pulcian manner, Byron began *Don Juan* in July, 1818; finished Canto I in September; and dispatched it to Murray. In December and January, 1819, he composed Canto II; enjoying the freedom of his new mode, he wrote with gusto of Juan's sea voyage, shipwreck, and idyllic romance with Haidée. Both cantos were the product of Byron's Venetian period, during the reign of the Fornarina and Byron's most extreme sexual indulgence. Joseph agrees with Robert Escarpit that Byron's "dissipations" in Venice were "a healthy re-immersion in common life."[31] His Boccaccian experiences had a salutary effect on his poetry, helping him to recapture something of the earthiness and vitality of Chaucer.

Meanwhile, the caution of Murray and the apprehension of Byron's "cursed puritanical committee" delayed publication of *Don Juan,* Cantos I and II, until July 15, 1819 — almost a year after composition had begun. Byron, who had fought with Murray and his "committee" to get it published at all, pinned his whole poetic future on *Don Juan.* He was convinced that it was good and knew his advisors thought the same but were fearful of it on "moral" grounds. He stoutly maintained that it was "the most moral of poems." "Born for opposition" as Byron declared himself to be, he was determined on publication for three chief reasons, as Miss Boyd notes: to reform the literary taste of his time in favor of Pope, to satirize hypocrisy, and to defend individual and political freedom.[32] In the end, he had his way. But even then the timorous Murray crept out with *Don Juan* without either the author's or the publisher's name on the title page.

The outcry against *Don Juan* was almost unprecedented. The extreme hostility of the reviews, allegedly on moral grounds, was actually along political lines, as I have detailed in my study of the contemporary reception of *Don Juan*.[33] The nadir of pejorative attack was reached in the Tory *Blackwood's Magazine,* which branded the author of the "filthy and impious" poem "a cool unconcerned fiend."

Undaunted, Byron spiritedly defended *Don Juan*. Determined to ignore the admonitions of his "Senate" and fearful publisher, he resolved to continue the poem in his own way. But the discouraging reports from London of critical virulence, public indifference, and poor sale slowed down Byron's *estro* in the composition of the next three cantos. Writing, revision, and publication of Cantos III, IV, and V occupied two years; III and IV were composed in the fall of 1819; V, in the fall of 1820, and publication came not until August 1821. Other factors in the delay of *Don Juan* were Byron's involvement with Teresa Guiccioli and the Gambas and with Italian Carbonari activities.

As the future of *Don Juan* looked increasingly dark — even though the poet was full of plans for its indefinitely extended continuation — Byron took up a different line of writing in his unending search for new and appropriate poetic forms. The writing of poetic drama on Classical principles occupied his attention throughout most of 1820 and 1821. "The melancholy story of neglect, misunderstandings, and cross purposes," as Miss Boyd calls it, finally ended in the belated publishing of Cantos III, IV, and V in August 1821.[34] Contrary to all expectations, the volume sold tremendously. But, ironically, Byron had just promised Teresa in July to discontinue *Don Juan* because she was distressed by its treatment of love. This apparent ill wind may have driven Byron full sail into the composition of *The Vision of Judgment* in a "triumphant burst of creative energy."[35]

But Byron had by no means given up *Don Juan*. Several factors brought him back to his major work. "John Bull's" *Letter to Lord Byron* urging him to "stick to Don Juan" as his best and most enduring work, Shelley's renewed encouragement, the unfavorable reception of his dramatic efforts which he had doggedly pursued, and his own conviction by 1822 that in his epic satire he had found his true forte — all these renewed his faith in *Don Juan* and impelled him to resume composition. This he apparently did by as early as April, 1822, in spite of Teresa's interdiction, her "embargo" being lifted later, in the summer, on the provision that *Don Juan* be "more guarded and decorous" than before.

Conspicuously flouting the stipulations of his "dictatress," Byron resumed *Don Juan* with Canto VI, the harem scene; finished VII and VIII by August; IX–XI by October; and XII by December, 1822. It was at this time that Byron withdrew from Murray, "the most timid of God's booksellers," and changed to John Hunt as his publisher. After a brief lull in composition of *Don Juan* in January and February, 1823, during which he wrote the *Age of Bronze* and *The Island,* Byron returned to his great satire and wrote Cantos XIII to XVI from February 12 to May 5, 1823. When he sailed for Greece in July, Byron took with him the unfinished fragment of Canto XVII. Rutherford calls this period from April, 1822, to May, 1823, "the most sustained creative effort of his whole life," proving that Byron had "at last come to full recognition of *Don Juan's* greatness."[36]

Don Juan genuinely grew and changed during the five-year period of its composition. Although the progress of its writing was irregular and frequently interrupted, owing chiefly to Byron's uncertainty as to the poetic form best suited to his genius, *Don Juan* does manifest development and enlargement of purpose. Beginning with Byron's partly facetious "I *have* no plan — I *had* no plan. ... Do you suppose that I could have any intention but to giggle and make giggle?" the underlying deep seriousness of the poet's satiric intention becomes increasingly manifest in the cantos following the longest break in composition, the fall of 1820 to the spring of 1822.

As Joseph comments, Byron's apparent intention up to the end of Canto V was to write an orthodox, mock-heroic poem. But after this long interruption in composition he chose to move his story from the plane of comic romance to comic realism. The realistic later cantos justify T. S. Eliot's appraisal as "the most substantial part of the poem."[37] Byron's Preface to Cantos VI, VII, and VIII declares explicitly the seriousness of his purpose; and Cantos VII and VIII contain his thoroughgoing satire of war and tyranny. By the time he had finished Canto XII he wrote Murray, "*Don Juan* will be known by and bye, for what it is intended — a *Satire* on *abuses* of the present states of society..." Another dominant theme of *Don Juan,* political freedom, receives increasing emphasis, not only in the author's comments and protagonist's actions, but in Byron's apparent intention ultimately to involve his hero in revolutionary activity. As for the ideological growth of *Don Juan,* I have endeavored elsewhere to treat it fully.[38]

As Calvert wisely concludes, "...the conception grew with the execution." "The combination of freedom and purpose is the key to *Don Juan.*"[39] The whole moves forward, as Swinburne observed, with the magnificent rhythm of the sea. The epic scope of the work enlarges as the strong current of Byron's satire sweeps forward. Concluding Canto XII, Byron announces he has finished the "introduction" and is ready to begin the "body of the Book." He promises twenty-four cantos, twice the Classical-epic number. His plans for unwritten episodes are not to be lightly dismissed as mere Pulcian whimsy. And the possibilities of increasing the dimension of his poem by digression and satiric commentary were virtually unlimited. Byron abandoned his epic poem only when the opportunity came to join the epic struggle for Greek Independence. Indeed, "The story of the making of *Don Juan,*" writes Miss Boyd, "is the story of Byron's declaration of independence. . . .It marks his gradual emergence into freedom from the trammels of his own former self. . . .Byron wrote and published his greatest poem in spite of the world."[40]

IV *Narrative Content*

Miss Boyd lucidly summarizes the content of *Don Juan* as that "vast arabesque of narrative and digression."[41] The narrative is important, Miss Boyd reasons, because Byron is trying in *Don Juan,* in contrast to his earlier verse tales, to add to a straight adventure story the psychological realism and intellectual substance of the novel. Important as the predominating digressions are to reinforce the narrative, Byron's principal themes are implicit in the story.[42]

The Dedication to Robert Southey, "Epic Renegade," was circulated in broadside but not published with *Don Juan* until 1833. The poet lumps Wordsworth, Coleridge, and Southey together as "Lakers"; distinguishes Scott, Rogers, Campbell, Moore, and Crabbe as the important literary figures; and exalts Milton as the consistent "tyrant-hater," who never would have bowed, like Southey, to Castlereagh, the "tinkering slave-maker."

In Canto I, Don Juan — reared in Seville by his strict and hypocritical mother, Donna Inez — has a bedroom-comedy, first-love affair at sixteen with Donna Julia, the young wife of Don Alfonso, and is shipped off on his travels. The ship is wrecked in Canto II; and Juan, after an agonizing ordeal of open-boat survival and cannibalism, is cast ashore on an island in the Cyclades and rescued by the lovely Haidée, daughter of the pirate Lambro. The idyllic love affair of the two ingenuous youngsters flourishes in Canto III until, in Canto IV, Haidée's father returns home unexpectedly, seizes the intrepid youth who tries vainly to defend himself, and sells him into slavery in Constantinople, leaving poor Haidée to die of a broken heart.

In Canto V, Juan and Johnson, an English soldier of fortune, are bought by a black eunuch and smuggled into the Sultan's harem; and Juan, arrayed as a girl is brought into the presence of Gulbeyaz, the harem queen, whose advances he spurns. In Canto VI he spends the night pleasantly with Dudu and the other harem maidens, only to be sentenced next morning to death by the sack.

From the comic romance of the first six cantos, Byron turns in Cantos VII and VIII to comic realism as he satirizes war and tyranny. Juan and Johnson, escaped from the harem, join the Russian army and take part in the bloody Siege of Ismail. Byron's pioneering, ultrarealistic treatment in poetry of the savagery, inhumanity, and futility of war and of the emptiness of military glory is vividly illustrated by Juan's experiences during the taking of Ismail in Canto VIII: he distinguishes himself for bravery and rescues the little Turkish orphan Leila. These cantos contain Byron's utter despite for wars of conquest, for the savagery of ruthless generals like Potemkin, and for "Christian" tyrants like Catherine of Russia. "For I will teach, if possible, the stones / To rise against earth's tyrants."

In Cantos IX and X, Juan is dispatched to the court of the Empress Catherine, "the greatest of all Sovereigns and Whores," wins her royal favor, sickens under her insatiable demands, and is sent on a secret mission to England. Here in the English Cantos, XI to XVI, Juan, considerably matured in discretion and worldly wisdom, encounters contradictions of the much-vaunted English freedom, such as English assistance in the restoring of tyranny on the Continent. Through the "double view" of hero and narrator, the poet launches a satiric attack in Cantos XII and XIII on the materialism and "cant" of English society, "Formed of two mighty tribes, the *Bores* and Bored."

With special emphasis on the "marriage mart," he implies the contrast between the loveless marriages of the *beau monde* and the true love Juan had experienced with Haidée. Here, in Cantos XIII to XVI, chronicling Juan's experiences in the Norman Abbey house-party, "the Pulcian epic merges into a social comedy," observes Joseph, and the complex story gradually unfolds, involving Juan with three sharply contrasted women, the sophisticated Lady Adeline, the amoral Duchess of Fitz-Fulke, and the pure and gemlike Aurora Raby.[43] Just when the story is about to develop into an entanglement for Juan which *might* have led to an analogue of Byron's own disastrous personal experience of marriage, and beyond (fruitless speculation!) to Juan's involvement in the French Revolution, the poem breaks off, unresolved, on a note of "sham-Gothic" comedy.

There could be no better or more appropirate way to conclude this synopsis than with Miss Boyd's inspired and incomparably felicitous metaphor for *Don Juan:* "It is a whole archipelago of narrative islands, some marshy and some firm and solid, floating in a vast sea of Byronic speculation."[44]

V   *Themes*

The grand and pervading theme of *Don Juan,* most critics agree, that is implicit in both the narrative and satiric commentary, is Nature versus Civilization. Early in the poem the hero experiences natural love with Haidée in a setting of pristine Nature, and the tone of both story and commentary is that of comic romance. The poem ends with the hero's complex experiences with sophisticated and sensual love in the effete milieu of English high society, and the pervasive tone is comic realism.

The aspects of this major theme are legion, especially when we add Byron's "lucubrations" — the almost endless list of his topics for digression. Suffice it to settle upon the four or five themes which Byron himself names at the end of Canto VIII, "Love — Tempest — Travel — War," all traditional epic themes. And, in Canto XIV, he tells us that he will take "A bird's eye view, too, of that wild, Society." The treatment of themes in *Don Juan,* as most critics agree, is both implicit and explicit. It is implicit, as we have noted, in the picaresque adventures of the hero; explicit, in the commentary of the narrator.

Love, in relation to the poem's grand theme of Nature versus Society, is perhaps the most important of the five named by Byron. His treatment runs the gamut from first love and natural love, through sensual love and selfish love, to fashionable love and love-less conventional marriage. Byron begins with the Don Juan legend only to depart from it and transform it, as Miss Boyd has noted, into a truthful treatment of love. In contrast with the socially cor-rupted Don of the myth, Juan is the Rousseauistic natural man whose love is instinctive and good. The sensual, selfish passion of the Spanish Don is the result of the corrupting influence of "un-natural" civilization.

Byron sharply contrasts the sentimental and erotically funny "first love" of Juan in Canto I with the idyllic natural love of Juan and Haidée in Canto II, which is a love frankly passionate, inno-cent, and unsullied by the hypocrisy of society. The poet describes the two young lovers in their pastoral Eden as "Half naked, loving, natural, and Greek." The eventual destruction of their idyll by the fierce conventions of Eastern society illustrates, in Miss Boyd's phrase, "the fragility of natural love in an unnatural world,"[45] and underscores the all-pervading theme of Nature versus Civilization.

The lovelessness of conventional marriage is implicit in Juan's adventures from the Donna Julia episode in Seville to the Lady Adeline encounter at Norman Abbey. It is, also, explicit in the satiric commentary throughout the poem. The poet's own unhappy experience of marriage prejudices him against all matrimony as the opposite of love. In marked contrast with the wholesome love of Juan and Haidée, the institutionalized "love" of marriage is hypo-critical, self-deceptive, artificial. Lovers are metamorphosed into "that moral Centaur, man and wife" in the "thick solitudes called social, haunts of Hate, and Vice, and Care."

In the court of Empress Catherine, "Russia's royal harlot," Juan experiences the seamiest side of love, selfish and sensual lust; and it so ennervates and sickens him that the insatiable Catherine is obliged to ship him off to England on a diplomatic mission. In English high society Juan encounters the loveless "marriage mart" which is truly immoral because the sexuality is hidden behind a hypocritical façade of convention. The designing love of Lady Adeline and the predatory love of the Duchess Fitz-Fulke are relieved only by the gemlike purity of Aurora Raby. Thus, *Don Juan* exhibits the whole spectrum of love — natural, sensual, selfish, conventional — and truly "glows with sexuality."[46]

Another epic theme, travel and tempest, has its analogue in the beginning of the Don Juan legend; but Byron uses it only as a point of departure and alters it fundamentally. The Spanish legend begins with seduction, escape, shipwreck, and rescue by an ingenuous girl whose kindness is rewarded by seduction. We have already noted the contrast in the realism of the shipwreck in Canto II and in the natural purity and integrity of Juan's love for Haidée. But, more important, Juan's travels have educative value by introducing the hero to modern societies and people and by fostering his human sympathy and cosmopolitan tolerance. Especially was this true of the effect of Greece on both Juan and Byron, as Miss Boyd perceptively observes. Byron was by no means the first British Philhellene, but he was probably the most influential. His deep interest was not just in Ancient Greece but in modern Greece and its future. Byron probably intended the hero of his epic travel-poem to die a champion of freedom in a revolutionary cause; and, appropriately and ironically, Juan first encounters "tyranny and slavery in Greece, the cradle of beauty and freedom."[47]

Of the two great epic themes, Love and War, "Love is the creating, War the uncreating principle of life," Joseph succinctly observes.[48] Byron presents a full-scale panorama of all the aspects of war in ultrarealistic detail, a pioneering and unique achievement in English poetry. As already stated, the treatment of the theme of war in *Don Juan* is one of the major departures of Byron's epic satire from the Spanish legend. In Cantos VII-VIII the poet mounts a concerted attack on wars of conquest and strikes his strongest blow for political freedom. By embroiling his hero in the Russo-Turkish War, Byron is able, both by story and commentary, to denounce the savagery, abysmal inhumanity, folly, and utter futility of war, and to illustrate most tellingly his major theme of Nature versus Civilization.

> So much for Nature: — by way of variety,
>   Now back to thy great joys, Civilization!   4
> And the sweet consequence of large society,
>   War — pestilence — the despot's desolation, . . .

The theme of war merges inevitably into the theme of tyranny which, in Byron's view, is inseparable from war and, in fact, is its primary cause. Heartless despots who rejoice in conquest and carnage, such as Catherine of Russia and Napoleon the liberator turned conqueror, are the objects of Byron's forthright attack. Likewise, by implication, George IV and Castlereagh come under condemnation as quietly sanctioning and as culpably condoning, if not actually conspiring in,the restoration of the old, reactionary dynasties on the Continent following Waterloo.

Finally, *Don Juan* concludes with satire, more explicit in the commentary than implicit in the story, of modern society in general and of England and things English in particular.[49] In the English Cantos Byron focuses his satiric lens on the *beau monde* of English high society with its artificiality, complacency, hypocrisy, and crass materialism. In sharp contrast with the unnaturalness of "civilized" society, Byron juxtaposes the Arcadian wholesomeness of the American frontier with Daniel Boone as the natural man and modern "noble savage." This juxtaposition is not a sentimental lapse on Byron's part but a genuinely felt emotional conviction of the fundamental opposition between Nature and Society, the general theme of *Don Juan*.

VI   *Structure and Style*

As we have seen in our discussion of the composition and growth of *Don Juan,* Byron's conception of his epic satire grew with the execution. His allegedly planless poem exhibits increasing plan and structure as it advances from the comic romance plane of the first five cantos to the plane of comic realism in the continuation. To be sure, *Don Juan* is a fragment, gigantic and unfinished, that lacks formal coherence. But the dominating personality of its author imparts a sustained emotional and intellectual tone that pervades and unifies the whole, despite the change from comic romance to comic realism.

The framework of the poem is dual: the time-framework (itself dual); and the narrative framework (dual or triple). The two times of the framework, readily distinguishable yet congruent, are Juan's "present," the world of 1790, and the narrator's "present," the world of 1820. In the narrative framework we are aware of at least two levels: the adventures of the hero; the narrator's commentary; and, sometimes, the digressions of the author, speaking in his own right.[50]

Joseph's analysis of the narrative devices of *Don Juan* is brilliant. The separation of himself from his hero, for which Byron had striven in *Childe Harold,* is achieved in *Don Juan* in the complete dissociation of hero and narrator, a division which allows the author simultaneous self-dramatization and self-detachment. He now perfects his "master device" of "showman-narrator." The narrator in Canto I is clearly Byron himself, and most of the digression is personal. With Canto VI, after the break in composition, and through Canto IX, the autobiographical references are greatly diminished; but they resume and multiply again in the English Cantos as Juan returns to England. Events in Juan's "present" and the "present" of the showman-narrator (Byron) become juxtaposed, as the narrator paints the panorama of English high society. Byron himself is the defeated and exiled "grand Napoleon of the realms of rhyme," and in the brilliant *Ubi sunt* stanzas in Canto XI he meditates with alternate sadness and amusement on the amazing changes in the *beau monde* since 1815.

Juan, the hero, has matured in worldly wisdom but is essentially the same in nature, experienced but innocent. The narrator (Byron) has aged and changed. The "pathetic-ironic contrast" is accentuated; and the "like-unlike relation of narrator and hero runs like a giant simile through the whole poem."[51] "As a matter of biographical fact," writes John D. Jump, "Byron evidently thought of himself as speaking with his own voice in *Don Juan....* This is a voice that defines him sharply and leaves him in sole command of the poem; and it is surely the voice of Byron himself as we know it in his letters and journals. . . ."[52]

Digression, comic, serio-comic, or serious; and commentary, playful or satiric, occupy approximately one-third of the entire poem, varying with different cantos from about one-fourth in

Canto I to seventy percent in Canto XII.[53] In his *Beppo* Byron had practiced successfully the stylistic device of comic digression. The Italian comic epic writers and Fielding and Sterne had provided Byron with the example of digression used for the author's comment on literature and life. The function and value of digression is apparent, that of simultaneously presenting emotional experience and commenting on it. Its dramatic function is that of providing the reader with a lively awareness of the narrator who interposes himself between the reader and the story. Digression supplies kaleidoscopic background against which the hero's travels and adventures appear in bold relief. The narrative is the sustaining element in the poem, the digression the ever-changing one, and the interplay between the two provides the mobility and vitality of the whole work.[54]

The very essence of the style of *Don Juan* is the deliberately lowered tone — the antithesis of the grand style. It has the easy-going laxity of ordinary conversation; it ingratiates itself by virtue of its casual and careless manner of "talking" about common everyday life. "As to *Don Juan,* confess, confess — you dog and be candid—," Byron wrote Kinnaird, "that it is the sublime of *that there* sort of writing — it may be bawdy, but is it not good English? It may be profligate but is it not *life,* is it not *the thing?*"[55] In fact, *Don Juan* has not one style but a "multiplicity of styles" or tones — what has been called the "medley" style. Grave, gay, serious, ludicrous, sentimental, laughing, ironic, cynical, urbanely naughty, wittily outrageous, unexpectedly twisting familiar figures of speech and infusing them with fresh vitality, and accomplishing all with the most ingenious rhyming imaginable.

"Don Juanism" is Miss Boyd's happy phrase for the variegated style of *Don Juan*. It stands in debt, as we have seen, to the Italian comic-epic poets, Pulci, Berni, and Casti, for its *ottava rima* verse form, its manner and mood, deliberate lack of coherent construction, length determined by the will or whimsy of the poet, variety of incidents and digressions, startling alternations of mood, and pervasive modernity of spirit. The rapid movement from romantic seriousness to burlesque, as Joseph points out, suggests a Chaucerian quality — "one has to turn back to Chaucer to find, in English poetry, the same movement between romance and burlesque, chivalry and bawdery, ideal and real."[56]

Perhaps the most conspicuous and ingratiating characteristic of the Juanesque style is the conversational and colloquial tone, first introduced into mock-heroic poetry by Pulci. "*Don Juan* should always be read," says Miss Boyd, "as if Byron were reciting it, impromptu, in an after-dinner company."[57] As we have already noted, *Don Juan* has much of the quality of Byron's letters and conversation: allusive, anecdotal, whimsical, genial, vivacious, pungent, frank, uninhibited. The ubiquity of these inimitable qualities of Byron's "very self and voice" makes the reading of his correspondence and collected conversations (thanks to Lovell), an unending delight.[58] This same "headlong volubility" (Miss Boyd) provides much of the fun of reading *Don Juan* and listening to the "suppressed laughter" in Byron's voice — the tone testified to by his privileged contemporaries.

That Byron was indebted, likewise, to a native colloquial tradition in English poetry is the persuasive thesis of Ronald Bottrall. He names Chaucer, Donne, Dryden, and Pope as predecessors of Byron in the use of the word order, rhythm, and vigor of colloquial English and in the devices of poetic anticlimax, figures and images in satiric progression, double meanings, epigrams, parody, and puns. Bottrall also points to the "Chaucerian skill" of Byron in the employment of mood-setting digression and to the "Chaucerian trick" of realistic dialogue at the very crisis of his narrative. Like Chaucer, again, Byron works out a technique "to sum up a society and an era."[59]

To these English authors and their work should also be added the stylistic contributions of Fielding and Sterne. The former supplied Byron not only with a model for his protagonist in Tom Jones, as previously noted, but also with suggestions for the showman-narrator device, the mock-heroic manner, and urbanity of style. And from the author of *Tristram Shandy* Byron must have learned to employ the deliberate digression, Shandean whimsy, and wicked humor.

The Italian *ottava rima* provided Byron with ample room for his "voluminous Muse," and its concluding couplet encouraged the recurring humorous sally and satiric descent to the absurd, as in the description of the kiss of Juan and Haidée:

> A long, long kiss, a kiss of Youth, and Love,
>   And Beauty, all concentrating like rays
> Into one focus, kindled from above;

> Such kisses as belong to early days,
> Where Heart, and Soul, and Sense, in concert move,
> And the blood's lava, and the pulse a blaze,
> Each kiss a heart-quake, — for a kiss's strength,
> I think, it must be reckoned by its length.   4

The flexible and versatile Italian stanza accommodates a great variety of stylistic devices.[60] A favorite of Byron's is the multiple simile in which a series of comparisons is attached to a single object, modulating one into another or progressively diminishing as in musical dynamics.[61] Again, there is the use of images to "define a state or situation surprisingly and exactly" which Joseph describes as "metaphysical" and which Ridenour calls the Byronic "conceit."[62] Striking examples are the image of Dudu, the harem beauty, as "a soft landscape of mild Earth" and the description of Lady Adeline as "frozen champagne." And, finally, there are the infinitely varied and always appropriate levels of diction — colloquial, literary, *haut monde,* Regency "dandy," and underworld slang.

Over, under, and throughout all appear and reappear the poet's two major myths or metaphors: the cyclical recurrence of Paradise and the Fall, and the Ocean image in which Empires rise and fall "but like some passing waves" and Man is but the foam floating on the eternal flux.[63]

We may agree, in part, with Rutherford's appraisal of Byron's sprawling comic epic which, he says, "became something of a large, loose, baggy monster, full of life, but lacking the concentrated power which comes only with organic unity such as we admire in *Paradise Lost* . . . or *Tom Jones*, . . ."[64] Yet Byron's pervasive ironic humor, satiric intention, and intense personality so suffuse the work that "une unité intime" (in Gendarme de Bevotte's phrase)[65] is achieved. "*Don Juan* is a literary cosmos, not a chaos," says Miss Boyd, "for the modulations of subject matter and style are so contrived that the whole is as solid and brilliant as a faceted diamond. The unifying force of Byron's consciousness is the fire at the center of it."[66] Whatever *Don Juan* lacks in polish and perfection it makes up in force, grandeur, and originality.

VII *Context*

Don Juan in Context, Jerome J. McGann's most recent book on Byron, is perhaps unique among Byron studies because it affirms that *Don Juan* is at once an apotheosis and a critique of High Romanticism and because it advances two highly original and important ideas: (a) Byron's conception of imagination as both a creative and analytic instrument, and (b) the importance and meaning of context as a field of knowing.[67] McGann's book is organized in terms not only of the "certain contexts of fact and idea which were important to Byron the man," but of "the ultimate condition of the masterwork for which he is, as a poet, most famous." These factors include "Byron's personal character," the "literary theory and practice which impinged upon Byron's developing ideas about literature and his own place in it," and the personal, literary, historical aspects of *Don Juan* itself.[68]

McGann confides that he did not begin to grasp the esthetics of *Don Juan* until he began to understand not only its composition, but also the complete background of Byron's life and art. He writes, "the analysis of style, form, and content became possible for me only *ex post facto,* specifically, after I had been able to see the poem in a context which clarified the esthetic questions." Context as a crucial factor in all meaning, McGann demonstrates, "is one of *Don Juan's* most important ideas, running through the poem as a recurrent theme but also bearing directly on the nature of the poem's style and form as well." "The context of *Don Juan's* composition helps to graph the essential qualities of the poem itself."[69]

Of the style of *Don Juan,* McGann points out that whereas "*English Bards* was written under the aegis of Juvenal.... *Don Juan,* on the other hand, was just as deliberately Horatian." Beginning *Don Juan* as another self-contained story in the manner of *Beppo,* Byron extended his poem into "a large-scale attack upon Romantic mannerism — at once a theoretical assault upon the enemy and a pragmatic illustration of what poets ought to be doing." The Horatian basis of *Don Juan* is indicated by the epigraph that Byron eventually gave to Cantos I–V from *Ars Poetica:* "Difficile est proprie communia dicere." The style of *Don Juan* became a blend of the conversational and comic manner of Pulci and Casti with the "plain style" or "Domestica Facta" of

Horace.[70] "*Don Juan,*" McGann writes, "was deliberately begun as an attack upon this Romantic stylistic revolution, and as a partial return to the poetic position and understanding of earlier and more traditional poets."[71]

This view does not indicate, McGann continues, "that *Don Juan* is not a Romantic poem, for it certainly is that; but it is to say that Byron's epic set out to save both past and present and to show that the understanding and attitudes of more traditional poetic minds were not so incompatible with Byron's age, or even so different. ....The purpose of the venture was to show what Romanticism was in danger of losing when poets 'systematically' turned their backs upon past poetic traditions."[72] Emphasizing that to describe the parallels between *Don Juan* and Horatian verse is not sufficient, McGann provides a succinct and lucid history of how "actual and pragmatic human virtues" were fostered by "those apparent dodos, rules of decorum and the theory of styles."[73] "The point of *Don Juan,* then," McGann concludes, "insofar as it is a literary manifesto, is to clarify the nature of poetry in an age where obscurity on the subject, both in theory and practice, was becoming rampant."[74]

Commentators on *Don Juan* have characteristically observed that the poem incorporates many styles and genres from the "plain" and "low" to the elevated; for this work ranges from Pulcian *reportage* and Horatian "Domestica Facta" to Juvenalian sublime. "Reading the poem accurately," McGann reminds us, "requires that we be alive to these shifts."[75] Byron's style is "formed out of a balance of styles," a balance sought from "a sense of the options they open up when used in a mixed or medley fashion."[76]

Such "shifts and transitions" Byron readily manages "because the whole point of the style of *Don Juan* is to explore the interfaces between different things, events and moods. *Don Juan* is a poem that is, in fact, always in transition.... a vast spectacle of incongruences held together in strange networks between the poles of sublimity and pointlessness. Transitions ... are the locus of all his opportunities."[77]

McGann concludes his analysis of the style of *Don Juan* by underscoring the poem's celebrated "openness." "When we speak of *Don Juan* as a poem of openness and possibility, we observe the literal basis of that quality.... It is the 'simple' style and 'factive' fact which can do or mean anything and which can be put to any uses. The style of *Don Juan,* in short, is what any poetic style ideally ought to be. It is perfectly serviceable, and the poem could no more do without it than it could do without the man who wrote in it.''[78]

As for the form of *Don Juan,* McGann observes that Byron definitely does not plan the course of events in his poem. Rather, "Byron positively suggests that his own method of writing is as unplanned as Juan's foresight is limited." Byron is committed to the unplanned form: "the fact is that I have nothing planned" (IV, 5), and this pattern of unforeseen consequences operates throughout *Don Juan.* "The result of a Byronic narrative in *Don Juan* is not even retrospectively a sense of probabilities but of achieved possibilities.... *Don Juan* is a network of such patterns."[79]

"The key of the form of *Don Juan,*" McGann tells us, "is the episodic method, where fortuitousness, not probability, is sought...."[80] In consequence, as far as criticism is concerned, "...*Don Juan* encourages almost endless commentary but frustrates almost every sort of formal analysis." This critical problem, McGann shrewdly observes, is directly related to the "polemical artistic purposes" of the epic: "Byron began *Don Juan* ... as a critique of the most significant poetic movements of his time.... *Don Juan* is Byron's practical illustration of the sort of critical stance Romantic poetry ought to take toward itself."[81] Byron denies Coleridge's famous postulate that the purpose of a narrative is to convert a series into a whole; he asserts that the purpose of his narrative is to convert the whole into a series. Byron does not think of form in terms of the Romantic metaphor of organic form, "presumed to be implicit in the process of creation"; instead, he agrees with Horace that "form in art is function, or the use to which the poem is meant to be put."[82]

McGann's distinction here is very important: "*Don Juan,* in this respect, constitutes a vigorous attack upon the Coleridgean, and generally Romantic, idea of the symbol as the mind's deepest form of insight.... The structure of *Don Juan* is based upon the structure of human talk, which is dialectical without being synthetic." The point of the poem is not "to give a sense or intuition of the whole"; by its "piecemeal" method, it intends "to prolong the experience, and the activity, of learning in the human world."[83]

Don Juan is unique, according to McGann, in that it "will allow us to formulate not an *idea* about itself but only ideas about what it is saying at any particular moment. *Don Juan* argues that while the world is the subject *of* our understanding, it is not subject *to* our understanding."[84] "History, tradition, and facts are Byron's ground not because Byron is a materialist, but because, for him, use and act are logically, and humanly, prior to ideas." In Byron's "radically empirical" view of the world, "Truth ... is in fact a multiplicity. The pursuit of Truth is only one of the ways men have pursued the truth."[85]

"Form in *Don Juan*," McGann concludes, "is what comes about.... It rarely emerges so that we can comprehend it, but mostly so that we can experience it."[86] Likewise, "The content of *Don Juan* is — what is there, which might be anything, and which is more than anyone could, perhaps, reasonably expect."[87] The flexible, digressive, episodic manner and structure allowed Byron unlimited expansion into "opposite and unplanned directions."[88]

In sum, Byron's "wide-mindedness" can best be understood by studying the style, form, and content of *Don Juan*.[89]

VIII *Satiric Significance*

Byron was fundamentally a satirist, from first to last. And, if the chief works of his middle period were Romantic, he never rejected Romanticism but absorbed it into his mature serio-comic mood and manner as a genuine part of the complex *mélange* of human experience. In *Don Juan* were united for the first time all the elements of his complex personality: his Romantic love of liberty, hatred of war and oppression, and endorsement of courage and passion; and his satiric sanity, strong common sense, *joie de vivre,* and ironic humor. Byron's mind remained fettered until he found the poetic medium best suited to his genius. *Don Juan* is a spiritual autobiography which reveals a mind in the making; and, we can agree with Calvert, this work "displays the personality of its creator more intimately than any other similarly great poem has ever done."[90] Byron does not hesitate to satirize his own earlier Romantic moods and poses — his "Byronic hero" alter ego — but he refuses to compromise his deep emotional convictions on things that really matter. The result is the achievement in *Don Juan* of a "double vision" which presents simultaneously Byron's comic-realistic view of human experience and his own mature self-knowledge.

In his pioneering study of Byron as a satirist in verse, Claude M. Fuess maintained that Byron's broader satire was "essentially shallow and cynical" and that Byron "took no positive attitude towards any of the great problems of existence."[91] The recent view of William H. Marshall is relevant here: "*Don Juan* should be regarded as a vast literary joke ... humorous in its means but, beneath the clownish leer, serious in its implications." "It is not," he continues, "satire, for it ultimately offers, in its description of the absurdities of the real, no suggestion of the ideal."[92] Now, as we know, Byron very definitely avowed his purpose in *Don Juan* to be "a Satire on abuses of the present states of Society. . ." And it is possible to distinguish the objects and to appraise the positive significance of his satire, as I have shown in an earlier study.[93] To do so is to absolve Byron of cynicism and to reveal his awareness and appreciation of the ideal as well as the real. As McGann wisely observes in his *Fiery Dust,* "In the end, his poetry embraces alienation, skepticism, constant change, as it were by necessity, and attempts to show how man achieves a Godlike sovereignty (or a childlike innocence) even in a 'waste and icy clime' (*Don Juan* VII,2).[94]

"Cant" is the keynote of Byron's satirical attack in *Don Juan.* "Cant" has been well defined by Joseph as "the discrepancy between the moral ideal and the human fact."[95] Byron's satire of "cant" — of pretense and falsity — proves his awareness and appreciation of the real and the true. "Cant" is pretense, both emotional and intellectual; self-deception is its essence. Byron does not deny the validity of real emotions and genuine moral principles. His habitual juxtaposition of the petty and heroic, the base and virtuous, is designed to represent the startling proximity in human nature of virtues and vices and to emphasize Byron's profound conviction that "words should be congruent with things, principle with practice."[96]

The chief objects of Byron's satiric attack in *Don Juan* are war and despotism and the falsity and corruption within modern social institutions. It is important to reiterate here that Byron's realistic portrayal of war is quite unique in English poetry.[97] He foreshadows the realism of the leading British poets of World War I — Edmund Blunden, W. W. Gibson, Robert Graves, Wilfred Owen, and Siegfried Sassoon — but surpasses them in the wide-ranging comprehensiveness of moods, authenticity of tone, and depth of his moral judgment. And this characteristic is all the more remarkable when we consider that Byron's near-professional display of military knowledge and remarkable understanding of war conditions and psychology proceeds from no first-hand experience of war on Byron's part. "He is the first really militant anti-militarist in English poetry," declares G. Wilson Knight. And he asks, "Was he perhaps groping after some wider recognition of the powers of love as an alternative to a world distraught by tyranny and slaughter? It is possible."[98]

For Byron, war and tyranny are inseparable. Byron's revolutionary fervor is genuine in his condemnation of England for her responsibility in the restoration of old dynasties and the support of reactionary governments. He exerted the wide-ranging influence of his satiric power against the prevailing spirit of oppression and political reaction which permeated Europe after Waterloo. Indeed, Byron has been said to have originated the radical campaign against European political reaction and the Holy Alliance. As the late Professor John Jump has truly said, "Byron's is a representative voice of this age of revolutions."[99] "For Byron's reputation was more than merely British. It spread rapidly over the whole of Europe and throughout the English-speaking world." "Byron's self-sacrifice in the cause of Greek independence deeply affected public opinion throughout Europe. Without it, the British, French, and Russian navies might never have united in the same cause at Navarino in 1827."[100] In short, in *Childe Harold* IV and especially in *Don Juan,* Byron became in the nineteenth century the "trumpet voice of Liberty" and the acknowledged champion of Freedom.[101]

It has been asserted that Byron's views on domestic politics are ambivalent and confused when compared with the lucidity and cogency of his satiric attacks on foreign despotism. Rutherford maintains that Byron shows surprisingly little concern with English domestic concerns, political and social, and he attributes this to the understandable ambivalence of his attitude toward England and things English — his genuine concern for reform and his ineluctable loyalty to his aristocratic class.[102]; but a differing view has recently been expressed by William Ruddick. When speaking of *Don Juan,* Ruddick eloquently writes that, "Above all, the Byronic narrator is now a man conscious of his relationship to the moral and psychological traditions of a living, European, Liberal and still developing culture. Against this stands the narrow parochialism of English Society and it is into the dark places of Regency society and the Regency psyche that Byron casts his warm, clear European light."[103]

But it may be reasonably maintained that Byron's social satire is essentially consistent — whether of domestic oppression or foreign tyranny. The fundamental consistency of Byron's social and political criticism is readily demonstrable, as Wilfred S. Dowden has convincingly shown in his definitive study of this matter.[104] Byron, ever a political realist, was ready to make limited compromises; and he had the pragmatist's readiness to undertake whatever practical task lay ready at hand. As a youthful Parliamentarian in his London years, Byron championed the Framebreakers as victims of an unjust social and industrial system, protested the inequities accorded Catholics and Irish, and associated himself with the Reform movement. There is no reason to doubt the sincerity of his avowals of willingness to "join up" with the "Reformers" if it came to revolution in England. In the post-Waterloo period of genuine English alarm over the danger of domestic revolution, Byron was actually feared as a possible leader of open rebellion. Later, in Italy, he enlisted his best efforts in the Carbonari plots against Austrian overlordship; and he made his final commitment in the Greek struggle for freedom from Turkish tyranny.

Eventually, and inevitably, Byron left the field of literature — of moral correction through satire — and entered the field of moral action. Byron, the poet, rising with such urbanity and triumph over the limitations of Byron, the man, is truly, as Miss Boyd says, "the final act in the drama . . . which makes the drama a tragedy in the true sense."[105]

Byron, a true satirist in the Classic and Augustan sense, has a firm moral framework and perspective from which to judge the objects of his satiric attack, whether war, tyranny, or social abuses. Clearly, he does concern himself with the great problems of human existence, and the fundamental import of his satire is positive. *Don Juan* is essentially an affirmative poem. Byron exalts, either explicitly or implicitly, the indestructibility of the human spirit, the creative power of human love, and the supreme importance of personal and national liberty. As an epic-satire of all that obstructs human freedom, *Don Juan* represents, truly, the flowering of Byron's essentially satiric genius.

IX   Byron's Contribution

Among the five major Romantic poets — Wordsworth, Coleridge, Keats, Shelley, and Byron — Byron is unique. He did not share with the others the exalted conception of the poetic imagination as the medium of revelation of ultimate truth. It was impossible for him to believe long in the benevolent naturalism of Wordsworth or to accept Shelley's faith in the perfectibility of man. Coleridge's abstruse thought was beyond Byron's grasp, though his intelligence was acute and logical; and the visionary insight of Keats was foreign to his experience. Augustan in his allegiances, naming Pope as his master, Byron was fundamentally a Romantic — albeit a Romantic paradox.

One of Byron's most conspicuous differences from his fellow Romantics was his unique concept of Imagination. Jerome McGann, in his brilliant study of Byron's masterpiece, *Don Juan in Context,* advances a new and original understanding of Byron's concept of imagination as essentially critical and analytic. "Like the other Romantics, he was in quest of something which seemed to him to have been lost. For Wordsworth, Coleridge, and Southey, the age seemed to have lost its essential spiritual heritage, and they sought to recover it through Imagination...."[106] But this concept of "Imagination as a new Absolute," the medium of revelation of ultimate truth, was the object of Byron's attack. McGann in his final chapter, "Byron and the Truth of Imagination," summarizes and synthesizes Byron's mature understanding of the meaning and function of Imagination.[107]

"The whole point of *Don Juan,*" McGann writes, "was to attack the 'Romantic' position especially."[108] Wordsworth and Coleridge were right in insisting upon the importance of the individual and the imagination to all of life, but they were wrong in thinking of life in purely inward and personal terms. "*Don Juan* is constantly trying to remind Byron's contemporaries, and us, that the meaning of events passes beyond human perception because the contexts of events are always larger than our own awareness. Insisting upon the primacy of the Imagination, we become less imaginative, more self-absorbed, Lake-locked."[109] Byron shows us that "life is the measure of imagination, not vice versa.... Imagination is part of the human world, not its defining idea. The human world exists as history, tradition, and facts before it ever can begin to exist as will or idea." Imagination is only one of the "ways men have developed for dealing functionally with the contexts in which they find themselves. For Byron, this often means the construction of imaginative systems which exposed the fact, and importance, of context itself."[110]

In glaring contrast with Keats, for whom "Imagination *was* Truth," for Byron "the truth of Imagination" was the truth, or truths, which poetry could bring to light with the aid of imagination. "The subject (truth) of poetry," McGann writes, "was not the poetic process itself — truth as imagination, in the Romantic formulation — but the human world of men and women in their complex relations with themselves, each other, and their environments, both natural and cultural."[111]

Consequently, Byron's idea about imagination may now strike us, "the late inheritors of Romantic ideas about poetry," as extremely novel, McGann continues, because we tend to equate imagination with creativity. For Byron, the imagination was creative only as the source of the poet's invention, as one of the poet's tools, as a means to an end. "The ultimate purpose of the imagination was not to create, as High Romanticism suggested, self-generated and self-justifying worlds and orders. Rather, it was to present fictive conditions in terms of which the human world would be more clearly revealed.... In the end, Byron's 'imagination' is not creative (in the Romantic sense), it is analytic and critical (in the philosophic sense). *Don Juan* is Byron's textual evidence for his position."[112]

"Byron's imaginings in *Don Juan* are directed toward clarifying the truth about the world, and especially toward expanding our perception of moral issues, problems, behaviors."[113] "*Don Juan,*" McGann concludes, "was an attempt to restore poetry to its proper place and functions, both for its own good and for the benefit of the world it was meant to serve."[114]

Byron's love of truth, virtue, and beauty was as deep and genuine as that of his fellow Romantics. But, where the others were "idealists" who wrote of mankind in the abstract, Byron was neither an idealist nor a cynic but a realist, writing of real men and women in the actual world. His sagacity and common sense impelled him strongly toward the achievement of some practical good. "Byron lived in the world," Bloom observes, "as no other Romantic attempted to live." "Byron's achievement in *Don Juan* is to have suggested the pragmatic social realization of Romantic idealism in a mode of reasonableness that no other Romantic aspired to attain."[115]

As the hopeful optimism and confident affirmation of Wordsworth and Coleridge ultimately diminished, and as the gap between private vision and the experience of reality widened for Keats and Shelley, Byron alone of the Romantics "found a way of expanding outward in his poetry" by virtue of his ironic detachment and comic vision. This is Edward E. Bostetter's persuasive thesis in *The Romantic Ventriloquists.* Byron demonstrated in *Don Juan* "how poetry could be vital and meaningful in the nineteenth century and still hold its pride of place as a social instrument."[116]

Byron's chief services to English literature are four: his "open poetry" style; his contribution to the colloquial tradition in English poetry; his narrative skill, second only to Chaucer's; and his celebration of "unadorned reality." In sharp contrast to the compresssion of modern poetry, densely packed and recondite, Byron's verse achieves its effect by ready communication and by sheer accumulation and exuberant expansion of thematic material, patterns, repetitions, and digressions. We must agree with Bostetter that the full appreciation of Byron as an artist comes only "through the accumulative impact of reading a lot of him."[117] Thus, Byron is again unique among the Romantics in his style. Lacking the "hewn" simplicity of Wordsworth's best lines, the lyricism of Shelley, the richness and intensity of Keats, and the wizardry of Coleridge, Byron's style has force, fire, and clarity. Spontaneous eloquence is its hallmark.

Byron's word order, rhythms, and vocabulary in his serio-comic verse are in the best English colloquial tradition from Chaucer to Donne, Dryden, and Pope. He enriches the tradition by the vigor, color, and variety of his "Juanesque" manner and mode. Again, in narrative skill and versatility, Byron has no superior in English poetry except Chaucer. Like his great predecessor, Byron uses Chaucerian devices and techniques, as Ronald Bottrall has shown, "to sum up a society and an era." Finally, the subjects of Byron's poetry are the large fundamental commonplaces of human experience, of life and death, growth and decay, man and nature. "Byron's apotheosis of the commonplace...," writes Bostetter, "is one of his great contributions to the language of poetry."[118] His strong sense of fact and entire emancipation from the inhibitions of his contemporaries led him to the celebration of "unadorned reality."

A new assertion about the coherence and wholeness in Byron's poetic canon has recently been made by several Byron scholars. Gleckner states in the introduction to his *Byron and the Ruins of Paradise* that he seeks "to see the poetic canon as indeed canonical, as elements in a fascinating history of struggle for form...."[119] McGann in his *Fiery Dust* demonstrates the basic continuity and natural development throughout all Byron's poetry.[120] And Michael Cooke advances in his *Blind Man Traces The Circle,* the "synthesizing approach" to Byron's corpus. "Basically it expresses the sense that Byron's poems transcend a collection and exist as a body of poetry, with a consistent and plausible articulation."[121] "This study," he concludes, "...has sought in effect to throw a single net over the apparent Proteus of the romantic period."[122]

Byron's "wholeness" in another sense — his philosophy of "Materiality" in which he celebrates the equality of flesh and spirit — has been strikingly enunciated by Jerome McGann. "From the very beginning he tried like all Romantics, to wed the divine and the natural orders, and eventually he decided that the two could only be fused if this world were regarded as a paradise. To achieve a state of infinite capability we must not move beyond the natural but into it. Materiality, the physical man, is the ideal, and his spiritually distinguishing element — paradoxical as it may seem — is precisely his physicality."[123]

"Byron stands between the two worlds [Italy and England] and takes the best of each: from England, moral earnestness and a sense of reality, from Italy, beauty, sensuality, and a sense of innocence. Thus he becomes the norm of the fulfilled man...."[124] "Byron's basic position," McGann concludes, "is a humanistic mean ... his pronouncements generally emphasize the corporeality of the spirit." They "remind us of the basic point, that flesh and spirit are inseparable." "...the ideal he celebrated was one that established an equality of value between flesh and spirit."[125]

Byron's larger contribution to the world scene is twofold: as a major satirist and as a perennial champion of freedom. A major satirist in both the Classic and Augustan sense, Byron starts from a framework and perspective of moral principles and launches one of the most concerted and effective attacks on human society in the history of satire. His social and political criticism, whether serio-comic or savage, is trenchant and telling in its denunciation of war, tyranny, and social hypocrisy. His major satiric device is ironic incongruity, the devastatingly funny but deeply serious juxtaposition of romantic illusion and "unadorned reality," the ideal and the actual. He purposes to cleanse the Augean Stable of Society as the necessary preliminary to the reforms envisioned by his optimistic but less realistic fellow Romantics.

Finally, Byron is a perennial champion of freedom who advocated the overthrow of social and political tyranny by active revolution. On his way to Greece he wrote:

> The dead have been awakened — shall I sleep?   4
>   The World's at war with tyrants — shall I crouch?
> The harvest's ripe — and shall I pause to reap?
>   I slumber not; the thorn is in my Couch;
> Each day a trumpet soundeth in mine ear,
>   Its echo in my heart —

The trumpet of Liberty would not let Byron sleep. Concern for the downtrodden and oppressed was ever "the thorn" in his couch. His independent spirit could find no rest except in struggle. "I was born for opposition," he had once declared in one of his shrewdest moments of self-analysis. If some elements of his life were absurd and unedifying, they dwindle into relative insignificance beside his undeniable virtues and positive advocacies. Our own twentieth century stands in need of Byron's warm humanity, therapeutic laughter, wholesome sanity, and political realism. His uncompromising independence of spirit, passion for freedom, and persuasive eloquence make Byron still one of the most effective champions of oppressed peoples and insurgent nationalities in the modern world.

Notes and References

Chapter One

1. Leslie A. Marchand, *Byron: A Biography* (New York, 1957), I, 4–12; 15–18.
2. *Ibid.,* 28.
3. *The Works of Lord Byron: Letters and Journals,* ed. R. E. Prothero (London, 1898–1901), V, 391; hereafter cited as *LJ.*
4. Marchand, I, 39.
5. Thomas Moore, *Letters and Journals of Lord Byron: with Notices of His Life* (London, 1830), I, 13.
6. *Ibid.,* I, 20.
7. Marchand, I, 56–58.
8. *LJ,* V, 450.
9. Marchand, I, 54–55.
10. *Ibid.,* 56.
11. *LJ,* V, 449–50.
12. Marchand, I, 61–62.
13. Moore, I, 38–39.
14. *Ibid.,* I, 39.
15. Marchand, I, 90n.
16. Thomas Medwin, *Conversations of Lord Byron, Noted during a Residence with His Lordship at Pisa,* 1821 and 1822. (Paris, 1824), I, 65–66.
17. Marchand, I, 80.
18. *LJ,* I, 19–22.

Chapter Two

1. *LJ,* V, 445–6.
2. Marchand, I, 107–109.
3. *Ibid.,* 125–26.
4. Andrew Rutherford, *Byron: A Critical Study* (Edinburgh and London, 1962), 16.
5. W. J. Calvert, *Byron: Romantic Paradox* (Chapel Hill, 1935), 76.
6. *LJ,* I, 147.
7. Marchand, I, 150–51.

8. *LJ,* II, 330.

9. M. K. Joseph, *Byron: The Poet* (London, 1964), 131.

10. R. C. Dallas, *Recollections of the Life of Lord Byron* (London: Knight, 1824), 33–36.

11. William H. Marshall, *The Structure of Byron's Major Poems* (Philadelphia, 1962), 27–28.

12. Calvert, 104–105.

Chapter Three

1. Marchand, I, 313n. (Erdman, "Lord Byron as Rinaldo," 192).

2. William A. Borst, *Lord Byron's First Pilgrimage* (New Haven, 1948). Fully records the first *Childe Harold* tour.

3. Marchand, I, 209.

4. Borst, 83.

5. *The Works of Lord Byron: Poetry,* ed. E. H. Coleridge (London, 1898–1904), II, 189; hereafter cited as *Poetry.*

6. Lecture by the Hon. Sir Steven Runciman on *British Philhellenes* at the British Council, Athens, Greece, November 10, 1964.

7. Marchand, I, 230.

8. *Byron: A Self-Portrait. Letters and Diaries, 1798 to 1824,* ed. Peter Quennell (London, 1950), I, 81.

9. *LJ,* II, 361. Also, Marchand, I, 258n.

10. *Poetry,* II, 1.

11. Moore, I, 273–74.

12. Marchand, I, 295 and note 2; 312–13 and note 5.

13. *Poetry,* II, 104; *Childe Harold* II, stanzas 9, 95, 96.

14. Marchand, I, 309.

Chapter Four

1. Marchand, I, 313–15.

2. *LJ,* II, 424–30.

3. David V. Erdman, "Lord Byron and Rinaldo," *Publications of the Modern Language Association,* LVII (March, 1942), 213.

4. *LJ,* II, 106.

5. Erdman, 193.

6. Marchand, I, 346.

7. Borst, *passim.*

8. Joseph, 14–15.

9. *Ibid.,* 20–22.

10. *Poetry,* II, 3.

11. Rutherford, 31.

12. *Ibid.,* 33.
13. Joseph, 23.
14. Peter Thorslev, Jr., *The Byronic Hero* (Minneapolis, 1962), *passim.*
15. Calvert, 112.
16. Graham Hough, "Two Exiles: Byron and Lawrence" in *Image and Experience* (London, 1960), 141.
17. Rutherford, 34.
18. Jerome J. McGann, *Fiery Dust: Byron's Poetic Development* (Chicago, 1968), 105.
19. Joseph, 27–32.
20. *Ibid.,* 17.
21. Terence Spencer, *Fair Greece, Sad Relic* (1954), 259. Also, Lecture, British Council, Athens, February 23, 1965.
22. Joseph, 18.

Chapter Five

1. *Lord Byron's Correspondence,* ed. John Murray (New York, 1922), I, 93–94; hereafter cited as *LBC.*
2. Marchand, I, 390n; "Reform" not achieved until the Reform Bill of 1832.
3. Paul G. Trueblood, "Byron: Champion of Freedom," Lecture at Pierce College, Athens, Greece, February 4, 1965.
4. *LJ,* II, 229–30.
5. Marchand, I, 395–96.
6. *Ibid.,* I, 403–404 and n. 4.
7. *LJ,* II, 293.
8. Rutherford, 35.
9. *LBC,* I, 218.
10. Marchand, I, 426.
11. *LJ,* III, 56.
12. Thorsley, *passim.*
13. Rutherford, 38–39.
14. Joseph, 44–45.
15. Marshall, 63.
16. Rutherford, 40–46.
17. Marshall, 40–71; Joseph, 50–55.
18. Ethel C. Mayne, *The Life and Letters of Anne Isabella Lady Noel Byron* (New York, 1929), 111–12.
19. Marchand, II, 483.
20. *Ibid.,* 503.
21. *Ibid.,* 506.
22. *LJ,* III, 175–76.
23. Erdman, 194.

Chapter Six

1. Marchand, II, 563–608; definitive account of separation.
2. *Ibid.,* 579.
3. *Ibid.,* 581–82.
4. *Ibid.,* 586–88.
5. *Ibid.,* 591–607.
6. Lady Blessington, *Conversations of Lord Byron with the Countess of Blessington* (London, 1834), 191.
7. The Poems of the Separation Byron later sent to Murray, who showed them to Byron's intimate friends. Lady Byron and Augusta also saw them.
8. Rutherford, 47.
9. Marchand, II, 608.
10. *Ibid.,* 609.
11. Calvert, 132.
12. Marchand, II, 617.
13. Ernest J. Lovell, Jr., *Byron: The Record of a Quest* (Austin, 1949). Presents Byron's view of nature.
14. Marchand, II, 632.
15. Rutherford, 69.
16. *Ibid.,* 67–68.
17. *Ibid.,* 74–75.
18. *LJ,* IV, 477.
19. Rutherford, 49–51.
20. Marshall, 72–74.
21. Calvert, 146.
22. Rutherford, 51.
23. Calvert, 146.
24. Joseph, 77.
25. *Ibid.,* 78.
26. Lovell, *passim.*
27. *LJ,* III, 365.
28. Robert F. Gleckner, *Byron and The Ruins of Paradise* (Baltimore, 1967), xvi.
29. *Ibid.,* 351.
30. *Ibid.,* 352.
31. Joseph, 81.
32. W. Paul Elledge, *Byron and The Dynamics of Metaphor* (Nashville, 1968), 7.
33. *Ibid.,* 8.
34. *Ibid.,* 12.
35. Rutherford, 64.

36. Gilbert Phelps, in *Byron: A Symposium,* Edited by John D. Jump (London, 1975), 53.

37. *Ibid.,* 75.

38. Rutherford, 65.

39. *LJ,* III, 359–60.

40. *Ibid.,* 364.

41. *LBC,* II, 19.

42. *LJ,* IV, 138.

43. Marchand, II, 656.

44. Samuel C. Chew, *The Dramas of Lord Byron* (Baltimore, 1915), 67.

45. *Ibid.,* 60–66.

46. Joseph, 104.

47. *LJ,* IV, 110.

48. Marshall, 97.

49. Calvert, 173.

50. *Poetry,* IV, 82.

51. Rutherford, 79.

52. Joseph, 106.

53. Rutherford, 88.

54. *Ibid.,* 91.

55. Joseph, 107.

56. Calvert, 143–44.

57. *Poetry,* IV, 104; *Manfred,* II, ii, 50.

Chapter Seven

1. Wilfred S. Dowden, "The Consistency of Byron's Social Criticism," *Rice Institute Pamphlets,* XXXVII (1950), 18–44.

2. Marchand, II, 676–77.

3. *Ibid.,* 699.

4. The terms "matrix" and "accretive" are used by Steffan and Pratt in the *Don Juan Variorum* (Austin, 1957) in order to distinguish original and later material.

5. Joseph, 83 and 85.

6. *Ibid.,* 83–86; Appendix B, 144–45.

7. *Poetry,* IV, 477.

8. Marchand, II, 701.

9. Gleckner, 297.

10. Joseph, 88.

11. *Ibid.,* 98.

12. Calvert, 149.

13. *Ibid.,* 151.

14. Elledge, 12.

15. McGann, *Fiery Dust,* viii.

16. *Ibid.,* 138.

17. Rutherford, 102.

18. Elizabeth F. Boyd, *Byron's Don Juan* (New Brunswick, 1945), 50–53.

19. Paul G. Trueblood, *The Flowering of Byron's Genius* (Stanford, 1945), 2.

20. *LJ,* IV, 71–72.

21. *LJ,* IV, 217–18.

22. Calvert, 93.

23. Joseph, 135.

24. Boyd, 46–47. See E. J. Lovell, Jr., *His Very Self and Voice: Conversations of Lord Byron* (New York, 1954), *passim.*

25. Rutherford, 107.

26. Boyd, 10.

27. *Ibid.,* 12.

28. Marshall, 168.

29. Rutherford, 122.

Chapter Eight

1. *LJ,* IV, 245.

2. *LJ,* IV, 260.

3. E. D. H. Johnson, *"Don Juan* in England," *English Literary History,* XI (June, 1944), 135–53.

4. Marchand, II, 764–65.

5. *LJ,* IV, 279.

6. *LJ,* IV, 283.

7. Teresa Guiccioli's manuscript, *"La Vie de Lord Byron en Italie,"* in Biblioteca Classense, Ravenna. Also, Origo, p. 12.

8. Iris Origo, *The Last Attachment* (New York, 1949), 44–45. Translation of Byron's Italian letters by the Marchesa Origo.

9. Leslie A. Marchand, "Lord Byron and Count Alborghetti," *Publications of Modern Language Association,* LXIV (December, 1949), 976–1007.

10. Origo, 79.

11. Trueblood, "The Contemporary Reviews of *Don Juan,*" in *The Flowering of Byron's Genius,* 26–72.

12. *LJ,* IV, 341–43.

13. *LJ,* IV, 350; See Origo, 112–13.

14. Marchand, II, 743–44; 744n.

15. Origo, 130–35 and *LBC,* II, 129.

16. *LJ,* IV, 396.

17. Marchand, II, 834.

18. *Ibid.,* 841–42; 842n.

19. *Ibid.,* 846.

20. Rutherford; 123.

21. Chew, *passim.*

22. E. D. H. Johnson, "A Political Interpretation of Byron's *Marino Faliero,*" *Modern Language Quarterly,* III (1942), 417–25.

23. Joseph, 114–15.

24. Calvert, 172; 162.

25. Joseph, 112.

26. Origo, 174.

27. Marchand, II, 858–59.

28. Origo, 185–86.

29. All that remained of the late seventeenth-century country home when I visited Filetto in 1964 was the fan-shaped flight of stone steps that once led from the salon to the wide lawn. Here, as a guest of the Contessa Cini, descendant of the Gambas, I learned of the deliberate destruction of the Villa Gamba in 1944 by the retreating Germans.

30. Origo, 204.

31. Marchand, II, 881.

32. *LJ,* V, 242–43. See Boyd, 39–41.

33. Alan L. Strout, ed., *John Bull's Letter to Lord Byron* (Oklahoma, 1947), 50–56.

34. Trueblood, 63–64.

35. *LJ,* V, 306–307.

36. Marchand, II, 918.

37. Joseph, 117–21.

38. Marshall, 136–54.

39. Rutherford, 92.

Chapter Nine

1. Origo, *passim.*

2. Marchand, II, 922.

3. *Ibid.,* 932.

4. Rutherford, 217–22.

5. Blessington, 390.

6. Rutherford, 231; 236.

7. *Ibid.,* 236. See also *LBC,* II, 203.

8. *Ibid.,* 237.

9. Marchand, II, 932.

10. *Ibid.,* 936.

11. Trueblood, 6–18; 145–53.

12. *LJ,* VI, 99.

13. Leslie A. Marchand, "Trelawny on the Death of Shelley," *Keats-Shelley Memorial Bulletin,* No. IV (London, 1952), 9–34.

14. *LJ,* VI, 155–56.

Chapter Ten

1. Michael Sadleir, *The Strange Life of Lady Blessington* (New York, 1947).

2. Blessington, 12.

3. *Ibid.,* 211–12.

4. Boyd, 162.

5. Origo, *passim;* Trueblood, 20–22.

6. Blessington, 67.

7. Origo, 337.

8. *Ibid.,* 344.

9. Marchand, III, 1087.

10. Harold Nicolson, *Byron: The Last Journey, April 1823–April 1824* (London, 1948).

11. Gamba Papers, Biblioteca Classense, Ravenna.

12. Marchand, III, 1094.

13. Nicolson, 135f; Marchand, III, 1100f.

14. Marchand, III, 1115.

15. *Ibid.,* 1116.

16. *LJ,* VI, 246.

17. Pietro Gamba, *A Narrative of Lord Byron's Last Journey to Greece* (London, 1825), 48.

18. *Ibid.,* 59–61.

19. Marchand, III, 1138–39 and Note 4.

20. Nicolson, 174.

21. William Parry, *The Last Days of Lord Byron* (London, 1825), 27–28.

22. *LJ,* VI, 326n.

23. Gamba, 192–93.

24. *Ibid.,* 221–22.

25. Nicolson, 244–45.

26. *Ibid.,* 231.

27. *Ibid.,* 108.

28. *LBC,* II, 292.

29. Parry, 123.

30. Julius Millingen, *Memoirs of the Affairs of Greece* (London, 1831), 132.

31. Marchand, III, 1219.

32. Millingen, 141.

33. Origo, 383 and note.

34. Marchand, III, 1226 and Notes, p. 143.

35. *Ibid.,* 1228.

36. *Ibid.,* 1236.

37. James A. Notopoulos, "New Sources on Lord Byron at Misso-longhi," *Keats-Shelley Journal,* IV (Winter, 1955), 31–45.

38. Marchand, III, 1231–34.

39. Origo, 384.

40. Doris Langley Moore, *The Late Lord Byron* (Philadelphia, 1961), 12–45.

41. Marchand, 1256n.

42. *Ibid.,* 1263.

Chapter Eleven

1. *LJ,* IV, 231.

2. *LJ,* IV, 245.

3. Boyd, 34–35.

4. *Ibid.,* 54–55.

5. Calvert, 193.

6. *Ibid.,* 194–97.

7. *Ibid.,* 198.

8. *LJ,* IV, 341–42.

9. Joseph, 184–85.

10. John Hookham Frere, *The Monks and the Giants,* ed. R. D. Waller (London, 1926).

11. Andras Horn, *Byron's Don Juan and the Eighteenth Century English Novel* (Swiss Studies in English,51 Bund, Basel, 1962).

12. Trueblood, 23–28.

13. Boyd, 55.

14. *LJ,* IV, 341–42.

15. Boyd, 83–111; 112–57.

16. Georges Gendarme de Bévotte, *La Légende de Don Juan* (Paris, 1911). Definitive treatment of the legend.

17. *Poetry,* VI, 11, note 2.

18. Boyd, 36–37.

19. Ronald Bottrall, "Byron and the Colloquial Tradition in English Poetry," *Criterion,* XVIII (January, 1939), 453.

20. Helene Richter, *Lord Byron* (Halle, 1929), 453.

21. Joseph, 163–64.

22. Trueblood, Lecture, Pierce College, Athens, February 4, 1965.

23. Boyd, 39–43.

24. *Ibid.,* 112–38.

25. *Ibid.,* 132–35; 148–50.

26. Trueblood, "Byron's Satire of War," 145–53.

27. Joseph, 172–73.

28. Calvert, 188.

29. Boyd, 43–44.

30. McGann, *Don Juan in Context* (Chicago, 1976), 10.

31. Joseph, 188.

32. Boyd, 14.

33. Trueblood, "Contemporary Reviews of Don Juan," 26–85.

34. Boyd, 20.

35. Rutherford, 135.

36. *Ibid.,* 137–38.

37. Joseph, 159; 156.

38. Trueblood, "The Growth of Don Juan," 1–25.

39. Calvert, 198; 201.

40. Boyd, 21.

41. *Ibid.,* 22–30.

42. *Ibid.,* 59.

43. Joseph, 155.

44. Boyd, 30.

45. *Ibid.,* 67.

46. Joseph, 242.

47. Boyd, 74.

48. Joseph, 248.

49. Trueblood, 127–45.

50. Joseph, 196.

51. *Ibid.,* 194–208.

52. John D. Jump, *Byron* (London, 1972), 111.

53. Joseph, 198 and Appendix C, 334.

54. *Ibid.,* 197–201.

55. Marchand, II, 823–24.

56. Joseph, 266.

57. Boyd, 46.

58. Lovell, *passim.*.

59. Bottrall, *passim.*.

60. Lovell, "Irony and Image in Byron's Don Juan," in *English Romantic Poets,* ed. M. H. Abrams (New York, 1960).

61. Joseph, 212–18.

62. George M. Ridenour, *The Style of Don Juan* (Yale Studies in English, Vol. 144, 1960), 138ff.

63. Joseph, 223–34; Ridenour, *passim.*

64. Rutherford, 141.

65. Gendarme de Bévotte, I, 270.

66. Boyd, 57.

67. McGann, *Don Juan in Context,* ix.

68. *Ibid.,* x.

69. *Ibid.*, 67.
70. *Ibid.*, 69.
71. *Ibid.*, 73.
72. *Ibid.*, 73.
73. *Ibid.*, 73 and 73–78.
74. *Ibid.*, 78.
75. *Ibid.*, 81.
76. *Ibid.*, 93.
77. *Ibid.*, 95.
78. *Ibid.*, 99.
79. *Ibid.*, 100–01.
80. *Ibid.*, 103.
81. *Ibid.*, 107.
82. *Ibid.*, 109.
83. *Ibid.*, 111.
84. *Ibid.*, 112.
85. *Ibid.*, 114.
86. *Ibid.*, 116.
87. *Ibid.*, 132.
88. *Ibid.*, 133.
89. *Ibid.*, 134.
90. Calvert, 210.
91. Claude M. Fuess, *Lord Byron As A Satirist in Verse* (New York, 1912), 215.
92. Marshall, 177.
93. Trueblood, "The Significance of Don Juan," 97–171.
94. McGann, *Fiery Dust,* 65.
95. Joseph, 284.
96. *Ibid.*, 285.
97. Trueblood, 145–53.
98. G. Wilson Knight, *Lord Byron's Marriage* (London, 1957), 287.
99. Jump, *Byron,* 135.
100. *Ibid.*, 184.
101. Trueblood, 13–19; 153–56.
102. Rutherford, 182–96.
103. William Ruddick, in *Byron: A Symposium,* Edited by John D. Jump (London, 1975), 127.
104. Dowden, *passim.*
105. Boyd, 158.
106. McGann, *Don Juan in Context,* 147–48.
107. *Ibid.*, 156–65.
108. *Ibid.*, 156.
109. *Ibid.*, 157.
110. *Ibid.*, 159.

111. *Ibid.,* 160.

112. *Ibid.,* 160–61.

113. *Ibid.,* 163.

114. *Ibid.,* 165.

115. Harold Bloom, *The Visionary Company* (New York, 1961), 265.

116. Edward E. Bostetter, *The Romantic Ventriloquists* (Seattle, 1963), 253.

117. Bostetter, *Selected Poetry and Letters of Lord Byron* (New York, 1951), xx.

118. *Ibid.,* xxiii.

119. Gleckner, *op. cit.,* xv.

120. McGann, *Fiery Dust, passim.*

121. Michael G. Cooke, *The Blind Man Traces The Circle* (Princeton, 1969), x.

122. *Ibid.,* xii.

123. McGann, *Fiery Dust,* 290.

124. *Ibid.,* 299.

125. *Ibid.,* 298.

Selected Bibliography

PRIMARY SOURCES
(only modern texts listed)

Byron: A Self-Portrait. Letters and Diaries, 1798 to 1824, ed. Peter Quennell, 2 vols. London: John Murray, 1950. Augments the Murray collection of letters and prints complete diaries.

Byron's Don Juan: A Variorum Edition. Eds. T. G. Steffan and W. W. Pratt. 4 vols. Austin: University of Texas Press, 1957. Definitive edition of text with analysis of composition and survey of criticism.

Don Juan by Lord Byron. Ed. Leslie A. Marchand. Boston: Houghton Mifflin, 1958. Entire *Don Juan* from text of E. H. Coleridge's edition, with ample notes.

Lord Byron's Correspondence. Ed. John Murray. 2 vols. New York: John Murray, 1922. Indispensable source materials.

Poetical Works of Lord Byron. Oxford and London: Oxford University Press, 1904. Oxford Standard Authors Series. Complete student edition.

Selected Poetry and Letters of Lord Byron. Ed. E. E. Bostetter. New York: Rinehart, 1951. Student edition, with perceptive critical introduction.

The Selected Poetry of Lord Byron. Ed. Leslie A. Marchand. New York: Modern Library, 1951. All of *Childe Harold* and large selection of other poems, except *Don Juan.*

The Works of Lord Byron: Letters and Journals, ed. R. E. Prothero. 6 vols. London: John Murray, 1898–1901.

Byron's Letters and Journals. Edited by Leslie A. Marchand. 11 Vols. London: John Murray; Cambridge: Harvard University Press, 1973-1980. Definitive edition.

The Works of Lord Byron: Poetry, ed. E. H. Coleridge. 7 vols. London: John Murray, 1898-1904.

Byron's Complete Poetical Works. Edited by Jerome J. McGann. 7 Vols. New York: Oxford University Press, 1978-1984. Definitive edition.

SECONDARY SOURCES

BABINSKI, HUBERT F. *The Mazeppa Legend in European Romanticism.*

New York: Columbia University Press, 1975. First comprehensive book-length treatment of the Mazeppa theme in the Romantic period, encompassing both Western and Slavic literatures.

BLACKSTONE, BERNARD. *Byron: A Survey.* London: Longman Group Ltd., 1975. A re-estimation of Byron on the basis of what he himself thought and said. Provocative.

BLESSINGTON, LADY. *Conversations of Lord Byron with the Countess of Blessington.* London: Henry Colburn, 1834. Perhaps the most interesting of all contemporary records.

BLOOM, HAROLD. *The Visionary Company.* New York: Doubleday, 1961. Fresh, perceptive reading of Romantic poetry.

BORST, WILLIAM A. *Lord Byron's First Pilgrimage.* New Haven: Yale University Press, 1948. The first *Childe Harold* tour.

BOSTETTER, EDWARD E. "Masses and Solids: Byron's View of the External World," *Modern Language Quarterly,* XXXV (1974), 257–71. Byron the only major Romantic to write in the Empirical tradition. The external world is the only reality for him. Authoritative.

————. *The Romantic Ventriloquists.* Seattle: University of Washington Press, 1963. Byron's demonstration of the vitality of poetry as a meaningful social art.

BOTTRALL, RONALD. "Byron and the Colloquial Tradition in English Poetry," *Criterion* (January, 1939), 204–24. Byron in the succession of older English poets from Chaucer on.

BOYD, ELIZABETH F. *Byron's Don Juan: A Critical Study.* New Brunswick: Rutgers University Press, 1945. Brilliant study of Byron's epic satire, sources, and "Don Juanism."

CALVERT, W. J. *Byron: Romantic Paradox.* Chapel Hill: University of North Carolina Press, 1935. Pioneering, general critical study of the poet as Augustan-Romantic. Excellent.

CHAPMAN, JOHN S. *Byron and the Honorable Augusta Leigh.* New Haven: Yale University Press, 1975.

CHEW, S. C. *The Dramas of Lord Byron.* Baltimore: Johns Hopkins University Press, 1915. First and authoritative study.

CLINE, C. L. *Byron, Shelley, and Their Pisan Circle.* London, 1952. Important account of Byron in Pisa in 1821–1822.

COOKE, MICHAEL G. *The Blind Man Traces The Circle: The Patterns and Philosophy of Byron's Poetry.* Princeton: Princeton University Press, 1969. A "synthesizing" approach to Byron's work as a consistent "body of poetry." Important.

DAKIN, DOUGLAS. *The Greek Struggle for Independence, 1821–1833.* Berkeley: University of California Press, 1973. Includes an authoritative discussion of Byron's role. Important.

DALLAS, R. C. *Recollections of the Life of Lord Byron.* London: Knight, 1824. Contemporary impressions, 1808 through 1814.

DOWDEN, WILFRED S. "The Consistency of Byron's Social Criticism," *Rice Institute Pamphlets,* XXXVII (1950), 18–44. Important study of Byron's political and social realism.

ELLEDGE, W. PAUL. *Byron and the Dynamics of Metaphor.* Nashville: Vanderbilt University Press, 1968. Investigates the primarily non-satiric works; finds that Byron's representative images reflect the essential dichotomy of human nature and dramatize the pathos and tragedy of mortality.

ENGLAND, A. B. *Byron's Don Juan and Eighteenth Century Literature: A Study of Some Rhetorical Continuities and Discontinuities.* Bucknell University Press, 1975. Places Byron again within the mainstream of English satire in comparison with Pope, Swift, Butler, and Fielding.

ERDMAN, DAVID V. "Lord Byron as Rinaldo," *Publications of the Modern Language Association,* LVII (March, 1942), 189.³231. Byron's Parliamentary career, 1812–1816.

———. "Byron and 'the New Force of the People,'" *Keats-Shelley Journal,* XI (Winter, 1962), 47–64. A newly conscious, increasingly articulate working class, a new confluence of poetry and politics, stimulate Byron's poetry of Reform.

ESCARPIT, ROBERT. *Byron: A Tempérament Littéraire.* 2 vols. Paris: Le Cercle du Livre, 1957. Discerns three Byronic modes, lyrical, rhetorical, narrative; the last is the superior form of Byron, the man of action.

FRERE, JOHN HOOKHAM *The Monks and the Giants,* ed. R. D. Waller. London: Murray, 1926. Introduction gives Byron's debt to Pulci and best survey of *ottava rima* imitations in English.

FUESS, CLAUDE M. *Lord Byron As A Satirist in Verse.* New York: Columbia University Press, 1912. Pioneering historical survey of Byron's satire, both Augustan and Italianate.

GAMBA, PIETRO. *A Narrative of Byron's Last Journey to Greece.* London: Murray, 1825. Moving account of Byron's last venture by his most devoted follower, Teresa's brother.

GENDARME DE BÉVOTTE, GEORGES. *La Légende de Don Juan.* 2 vols. Paris: Hachette, 1911. Authoritative account.

GLECKNER, ROBERT F. *Byron and The Ruins of Paradise.* Baltimore: The Johns Hopkins Press, 1967. Focuses on Byron's poems through 1816 and depicts him as a modern poet-prophet of doom with a consistent dark vision of the human condition after the Fall, the "ruins of paradise" upon which "all future building must take place."

GUICCIOLI, TERESA, "La Vie de Lord Byron en Italie" (unpublished 1,700-page manuscript in French). Gamba Papers, Biblioteca Classense, Ravenna. Revealing, if prejudiced, account by Byron's Italian mistress, probably the most influential and surely the most devoted woman in his life.

HORN, ANDRAS. *Byron's Don Juan and the Eighteenth Century English Novel.* Swiss Studies in English, 51 Bund, Basel, 1962. Byron's debt to Fielding, Sterne, and Smollet.

HOUGH, GRAHAM. "Two Exiles: Byron and Lawrence" in *Image and Experience.* London: Duckworth, 1960. Fascinating parallel study of the arch rebels of their respective periods.

JOHNSON, E. D. H. "A Political Interpretation of Byron's *Marino Faliero,*" *Modern Language Quarterly,* III (1942), 417–25. *"Don Juan* in England," *English Literary History,* XI (1944), 135–53. Both illuminate Byron's political views and conceptions of English middle-class society.

JOSEPH, M. K. *Byron: The Poet.* London: Gollancz, 1964. One of the few general critical studies of Byron. Excellent.

JUMP, JOHN D. *Byron.* Routledge Author Guides. London: Routledge & Kegan Paul, 1972. The social and historical context of Byron's life and times and the cultural and intellectual tradition in which he stands.

——. *Byron: A Symposium.* Edited by John D. Jump. London: Macmillan, 1975. Lectures in commemoration of the 150th anniversary of Byron's death under sponsorship of The British Council, The Byron Society, and Universities of London and Manchester.

KNIGHT, G. WILSON. *Lord Byron's Marriage.* London: Routledge, 1957. A different explanation of the Byron separation.

LOVELL, ERNEST J., JR. *Byron: The Record of a Quest.* Austin: University of Texas Press, 1949. Byron's vain search for a satisfying concept of nature. Important study.

——. *His Very Self and Voice: Collected Conversations of Lord Byron.* New York: Macmillan, 1954. Rich collection of contemporary impressions of Byron.

——. "Irony and Image in Byron's *Don Juan*" in *English Romantic Poets,* ed. M. H. Abrams. New York: Galaxy, 1960. Important study of style.

MARCHAND, LESLIE A. *Byron: A Biography.* 3 vols. New York: Knopf, 1957. Definitive and best biography of Byron.

——. *Byron: A Portrait.* New York: Knopf, 1970. Definitive one-volume biography by Byron's greatest biographer.

——. *Byron's Poetry: A Critical Introduction.* Boston: Houghton Mifflin, 1965. Most recent and authoritative critical appraisal of Byron's poetry.

——. "Lord Byron and Count Alborghetti," *Publications of the Modern Language Association,* LXIV (December, 1949), 976–1007. Byron in Ravenna.

——. "Trelawny on the Death of Shelley," *Keats-Shelley Memorial*

Bulletin, No. IV (London, 1952), 9–34. Authoritative evaluation by Professor Marchand.

MARSHALL, WILLIAM H. *The Structure of Byron's Major Poems.* Philadelphia: University of Pennsylvania Press, 1962. Perceptive, often ingenious, critical reading.

MAYNE, ETHEL C. *Byron.* 2 vols. New York: Scribner's, 1912; rev. 1 vol., 1924. Acute, understanding delineation of Byron's "enthralling humanity." Excellent biography.

———. *The Life and Letters of Anne Isabella Lady Noel Byron.* New York: Scribner's, 1929. Authoritative.

McGANN, JEROME J. *Don Juan in Context.* Chicago: University of Chicago Press, 1976. The importance and meaning of context as a field of knowing, in general and for Byron in particular, and the nature of imagination both as a creative and an analytic instrument.

———. *Fiery Dust: Byron's Poetic Development.* Chicago: University of Chicago Press, 1968. Demonstrates the basic continuity and development throughout all Byron's poetry as Byron explores and creates his own personality as he writes. One of the most important Byron studies of the twentieth century.

MEDWIN, THOMAS. *Conversations of Lord Byron, Noted during a Residence with His Lordship at Pisa, 1821 and 1822.* 2 vols. London: Henry Colburn, 1824. Controversial but very important record.

MILLINGEN, JULIUS. *Memoirs of the Affairs of Greece.* London: John Rodwell, 1831. Hostile account by Byron's doctor at Missolonghi.

MOORE, DORIS LANGLEY. *The Late Lord Byron.* Philadelphia: Lippincott, 1961. Fascinating account of Byron's posthumous influence on his wife, sister, and Hobhouse.

———. *Lord Byron: Accounts Rendered.* London: John Murray, 1974. Enlarges and modifies the reconstructions of the posthumous developments concerning Byron's fame which were Ms. Moore's main subject in her *The Late Lord Byron.*

MOORE, THOMAS. *Letters and Journals of Lord Byron: With Notices of His Life.* London: Longman's, 1830. First official biography. Moore was the recipient of Byron's eventually destroyed "Memoirs."

NICOLSON, HAROLD. *Byron: The Last Journey, April 1823–April 1824.* London: Constable, 1924; rev. 1948. Brilliant, objective account of Byron's Greek Adventure.

NOTOPOULOS, JAMES A. "New Sources on Lord Byron at Missolonghi," *Keats-Shelley Journal,* IV (Winter, 1955), 31–45.

ORIGO, IRIS. *The Last Attachment: The Story of Byron and Teresa Guiccioli.* New York: Scribner's, 1949. Major contribution to Byron studies. Indispensable new materials.

PARRY, WILLIAM. *The Last Days of Lord Byron.* London: Knight and Lacey, 1825. Reliable firsthand account by a staunch friend of Byron.

QUENNELL, PETER. *Byron: The Years of Fame.* New York: Viking, 1935. Brilliant account of poet's heyday in London.

————. *Byron in Italy.* New York: Viking, 1941. Lively interpretation of the Italian years.

RICHTER, HELENE. *Lord Byron: Persönlichkeit und Werk.* Halle: Niemeyer, 1929. Authoritative biographical-critical study.

RIDENOUR, GEORGE M. *The Style of Don Juan.* New Haven: Yale University Press, 1960. Analysis of Byron's major poetic and rhetorical techniques with relation to subject matter.

ROBINSON, CHARLES E. *The Snake and Eagle Wreathed in Fight.* Baltimore: The Johns Hopkins Press, 1976. New and perspicacious exploration of the interrelationships of Sheiley and Byron.

RUTHERFORD, ANDREW. *Byron: The Critical Heritage.* London: Routledge and Kegan Paul, 1971. Reprints major critical comments on Byron both from his contemporaries and from major Victorian critics. Corrects the misconception that the great critical issues concerning Byron's poetry approached solution only with the advent of "modern" twentieth century criticism. Excellent introduction.

————. *Byron: A Critical Study.* Edinburgh and London: Oliver and Boyd, 1962. One of the few general critical studies of the poet and his work. Excellent.

SADLEIR, MICHAEL. *The Strange Life of Lady Blessington.* New York: Farrar, Straus, 1947. Story of an important Byron contemporary.

SPENCER, TERENCE. *Fair Greece, Sad Relic.* London: Weidenfeld, 1954. The background of Byron's Philhellenism and his contribution.

ST. CLAIR, WILLIAM L. *That Greece Might Still Be Free: The Philhellenes in the War of Independence.* London and New York: Oxford University Press, 1972. Well-documented, interesting history of the Philhellenes in the Greek War of Independence.

STROUT, ALAN LANG, ed. *John Bull's Letter to Lord Byron.* Norman: University of Oklahoma Press, 1947. One of the few favorable contemporary reviews of *Don Juan.*

THORSLEV, PETER L. JR., *The Byronic Hero: Types and Prototypes.* Minneapolis: University of Minnesota Press, 1962. Definitive analysis of the ancestry of the Byronic Hero.

TRUEBLOOD, PAUL GRAHAM. *The Flowering of Byron's Genius.* Stanford: Stanford University Press, 1945. New York: Russell and Russell, 1962. Growth, contemporary reception, and satiric significance of Byron's masterpiece.

WEST, PAUL. *Byron and the Spoiler's Art.* New York: St. Martin's Press, 1960. Asserts Byron's compulsive exhibitionism.

Index